PRAISE FOR *THE CHAMPAGNE CEO*

"Having had the fabulous pleasure of working with Terri Eagle, I admire her phenomenal talents and energies as a manager. Her initials seem almost destined: T.E. could just as easily stand for Terrific Experiences! Tréssor Extraordinaire! Topissime Excellence!

The Champagne CEO is both fabulous and inspiring, sharing solutions and strategies that every CEO, coach, and manager should practice."

—Stanislas de Quercize

Board Member, BARNES International, Messika, Louboutin, Fondation Rémy Cointreau

Founder & CEO, SAVIH Family Office

Former CEO, Montblanc France, Montblanc USA

Former CEO Cartier France, Cartier USA, and Cartier International

Former CEO Van Cleef & Arpels International

Former Président, Richemont France

"Having worked closely with Terri Eagle, I can attest firsthand to her incredible skills as a CEO ... she has it all: great leadership with the uncanny ability to build a strong and fully committed team. Her ability to seek out the best (and often unexpected) talents that are required for a true leader has yielded tremendous success for all of the companies for which she has worked. *The Champagne CEO* is a must read for anyone who aspires to be the best in class, in whatever field they may work."

—Timothy Corrigan

Designer

"From Terri's early days at Pizza Pete to current Morilee CEO, her growth and success have been awe-inspiring to me. As her best friend of fifty years, I have seen her rise through life's challenges and triumphs. Cheers to *The Champagne CEO*!"

—Lael Paul, MD

"An insightful and captivating narrative from a masterful businesswoman and CEO on how to achieve exponential growth in business. Terri's journey is both deeply inspiring and thought-provoking, leaving me eager to integrate her ideas into the core of my own business strategy."

—Susie Kimball

Executive, Luxury Goods

"In this insightful and inspiring book, Terri Eagle reveals the winning combination of sharp business strategy and heartfelt leadership that has propelled her to the top. Her strategic business wisdom and unmatched sales acumen, coupled with genuine kindness and respect for those around her, lays a new groundwork for success in today's corporate world. This is a must read for anyone looking to break barriers, shatter glass ceilings, and lead with confidence while driving exceptional results."

—Claire Gilvar

Director of Corporate Engagement, Fashion Institute of Technology Foundation

"I've known Terri Eagle for about six years, and as a bridal and special occasion salon owner, I've never met anyone quite like her. Her superpower is her ability to listen, lead, and deliver. In an industry that was really quite stale, she really stands out with authenticity and her drive to offer her customers so much more than they expect. I am lucky enough to know her on a professional and personal level, and *The Champagne CEO* gives readers a refreshingly easy guide on how to challenge yourself to be your best self. A must read for any leader in life and in business."

—Steven Blechman

"Terri Eagle has masterfully woven together the golden nuggets from her early life lessons and the key decisions that have fueled her remarkable success as a CEO across multiple industries. This book is a must read for anyone looking for insights and the inspiration to face challenges head-on as they embark on their own journey towards greater self discovery, self belief, and career growth. In short, it's a powerful playbook, broken down in simple and practical steps for how to lead a successful life and reach one's full potential."

—Marnie McBryde

Founder, McBryde&Partners, Inc.

Career Advisory and Executive Search

"*The Champagne CEO* is an inspiring read that captures the essence of leadership, success, and the art of balancing ambition with authenticity. As a business colleague, I've had the privilege of working with Terri Eagle and have seen the principles she has laid out in this book come to life. Whether you're climbing the corporate ladder or seeking to refine your leadership style, this book provides a road map for thriving in today's fast-paced business world. It's a must read for anyone aiming to lead with purpose and passion."

—Lynn Tesoro

Strategic Consultant, Brand & Communications Strategy; Founding Partner of HL Group

"In *The Champagne CEO*, Terri Eagle offers business owners the opportunity to learn from an expert with a proven track record in starting and building successful businesses. Her shared vision and wisdom offers all business owners the guidance and insight they need."

—Candy Udell

President, London Jewelers

"Terri Eagle is a true leader. In *The Champagne CEO* she demonstrates her humility, empathy, how she quickly recovers from difficulties, how she builds a winning team, but most of all how she's trusted by her colleagues and clients.

Ms. Eagle presents real life examples so you can hone your skills. *The Champagne CEO* is a must read for all managers who aspire to greatness."

—Amy R. Churgin

Terri Eagle is an exemplary leader who has earned her position through her expertise as a brand builder, her customer-centric approach, and her passion for driving revenue growth across multiple industries. As "The Champagne CEO," her authentic curiosity and insightful perspectives are both thoughtful and highly relevant in today's dynamic business and social landscape. Successful leaders like Terri inspire and motivate their teams with a clear sense of direction, purpose, and vision. They empower others by sharing their knowledge, wisdom, and experiences. For these leaders, leadership is not just a role—it's a calling that drives them to uplift and elevate those around them.

—Timothy Boerkoel

Managing Director and Founder of The Brownestone Group

The CHAMPAGNE CEO

TERRI EAGLE
The
CHAMPAGNE
CEO
A SPARKLING JOURNEY OF SUCCESS
THROUGH COURAGE, CONFIDENCE,
AND COLLABORATION
Forbes | Books

Published by Forbes Books, Charleston, South Carolina.
An imprint of Advantage Media Group.

Printed in the United States of America.

10 9 8 7 6 5 4 3 2 1

ISBN: 979-8-88750-569-5 (Hardcover)
ISBN: 979-8-88750-570-1 (eBook)

Library of Congress Control Number: 2024924668

Cover design by Matthew Morse.
Layout design by Ruthie Wood.

To my fabulous husband, Bart Eagle, who has truly given me all the love, support, beautiful memories, and continued great adventures for more than thirty years. Bart, you give me the wingspan to fly like an Eagle! What a lucky lady I am to have you in my life! Love you …

XOXOXO

CONTENTS

ACKNOWLEDGMENTS

Cheers!

The top champagne toasts go to my dear family: my husband, Bart; my dad, Bill; my mom, Neva; Kristi; Laressa; Carol and Alan; Jason and Alanna; Jasper; Pearl; Lindsay and Robbie; Ellie; Benjamin; Jane; Randy; Lisa and Howie; Martha; and the best grandparents, Georgia and Leo, smiling from heaven, holding hands with my wonderful dad; Uncle Gordie; Aunt Pat; Cynthia; Dobbie; Herb; and Bob.

Cheers to my fur babies: in puppy heaven, Nikki, sixteen, and Zoe, twelve, as well as new puppy Kazzy, two—the best, loving, and fun pups!

Cheers to my fabulous friends over so many years: my bestie Lael Paul; KX; Susan Pomerantz and Debbie Miller; Lou and Donna Cona; Ali Cona; Amy and Gary Churgin; Alan Dubow and Holly Hasbrouck; Michelle and Andy Levine; Marnie and Jackson McBryde; Chet and Susan Borgida; Molly and Rob Kuffner; Hannah and Grace Kuffner; Carol Burger and Steve Lassoff; Mica and Russell Diamond; Andy and Patsy Boyland; Bill Mintz; Toni Haber; Merryl and Orrin Sherman; Susan Pikitch and Michael Giobbe; Caryn Hemsworth and John Cuccianno; Deb Klemm; Maureen Callahan and John Champagne; Madie Polyck; Tim Boerkoel; Timothy Corrigan; Christine Rubino and Steve Albucher; Greg Paul; Ethan Paul; Mason Paul; Dr. Jeffrey Fisher; Dr. Benjamin Cheney; Hal Goldstein; John Mitchell; Martin Watters; Robert Obradovic; Nick Arrojo; Gina Arrojo; Julie Porter; Gene Casey; Gary and Elaine Friedman; Sheila and Paul Minarsky; Faigie and David Richman; Joshua Siegel and Judith Peterson; Jack and Tracy Levin; Steven and Rebekah Blechman; Rebecca Kimura; Vasily and Tery Kafanov; Michaela Eulberg; Sande Finkel; Lisa Stone; the Bishop family; Jayne Pilner; and Roxie.

Cheers to my career dream team players and lifelong career friends over the years: Claire Fletcher Gilvar; Deborah Klemm; Victor Boccarossa; Lauren Lipschutz; Carol Pennelli; Janet Hayward; Tracy Squillante; Danielle Twersky; Carl Barbato; Maria Valim; Michael Schoenbart; Mike Spezialetti; Susie Kimball; Dawn Pearson; Cathy Fatta-March; Evert DeGraeve; Scott Vogel; Rosanna Sarcona-Doherty; Kate Talbot; Carrie Niese; Michael Cosentino; Steve Blanz; Katie Kinsella; Dara Caponigro; Paul Arasi; Toby Goldstein; Emily Lohrman; Fabrizo Cocchiano; Greg Tupe; Molly Kuffner; Surim Campos; Suly Yu; Aliea LaRocca; David and Margaret Allen; Tracy Spraetz; Elise Gibson; and Alaina Basden.

Cheers to: top CEOs, executive vice presidents, and business leaders—I have had the pleasure to know you, your businesses, and your leadership skills. I gained so much experience, knowledge, and support over the years! Thank you all so much!

Cheers to: Stanislas de Quercize; Sybil and David Yurman; Evan Yurman; Michael Gould; Tony Spring; Karen Katz; Ron Frasch; Jennifer DeWinter; Lisa Kazor; Howard Feldman; Tim Braun; Mark and Candy Udell; Andy Johnson; Steve Polacheck; Ed Bridge; Hal Taylor; Jenefer Lass; Tom Kennedy; Timothy Corrigan; Dara Caponigro; Laura Pomerantz; Tom Milillo; Mihir Bhansali; Eva Sideman; and Bob Wichser.

Cheers to my fabulous career marketing partners along the way (Wow! Thank you all!):

- Lou Cona; Amy Churgin; Tom Florio; Guilio Capua; Diane Mattioli; Linda Kloner; Pat McGirl; and the awesome Condé Nast group—best ever!
- Lynn Tesoro; Hamilton South; and David Lipman—marketing mavens!
- Steve DeLuca; Michael Clinton; Nina Lawrence; Steven Binder; Gail Day; Lisa Hughes—awesome publishing leaders.

Cheers to new business friends I'm enjoying along the career journey:

Jane Heflin, the National Bridal Market Chicago executive director; Rachel Jo Silver, Love Stories; Matt Hertz, Albasari Caro, and Jose Suarez of Barcelona Bridal Fashion Week; Emily Mercer, WWD women's fashion market editor; and Lili Blechman.

None of this would be possible without the number one, exceptional, and outstanding Forbes team! *Wow*, what an amazing group of professionals to work with! I'm so proud to know you all and feel so lucky!

Cheers and thank you from the bottom of my heart to:

- Rachel Hartman, my ghostwriter—thank you for placing your heart and soul into passionately capturing my story! All along the way, you took the time, the care, and tremendous enthusiasm to make it all come together so beautifully. Not only are you an inspiration yourself, but you are also my new friend. I feel so very thankful to know and cherish you in my life.

- Lauren Steffes, developmental editor—thank you for being such a great cheerleader and making every step a dream come true. You are a very special lady!
- Shandi Thompson, authority advisor—I deeply appreciate your support all along the way. You are a wonderful partner, always so kindly checking in!
- Elizabeth Brueggemann, production editor—thank you for keeping it all on track with tremendous grace and professionalism to coordinate so many important pieces! Always keep smiling!
- Chase Patterson—thank you for asking me to join the prestigious Forbes Authors group!
- DeVasha Lloyd, thank you soooo much!
- Heidi Scott, special thank you!
- Olivia Tanksley and Katie Walter, thanks a bunch!
- Miguel Casellas-Gil, leader of magnificent press!
- Matthew Morse, thank you for the cover design; you are such a pleasure to work with! Exceptional artist!
- Corrin Foster, number one to make a promotional CEO toast!

FOREWORD

LOU CONA, FORMER PRESIDENT CONDÉ NAST MEDIA GROUP

Luxury goods manufacturers and premium media brands of the late twentieth century have had a lot in common—big budgets, big audiences, and even bigger personalities at their respective helms. Though festooned with the glitz of Hollywood parties, power lunches and black cars, those budgets, audiences, and personalities bring with them, shall we say, an inflated sense of urgency and competition that, while imperative to building something of impeccable quality, also makes it difficult to foster beneficial working relationships.

Very often people are led around in circles, not by any malicious whim—they're yes'ed out of the room in order to protect feelings, or feedback is vague due to operational ineffectiveness.

But as the cliche goes, it doesn't cost anything to be nice. Sure, sometimes it hits your P&L as an "entertainment" or "gift" line, but in general, treating colleagues, clients (and in some cases, their partners) with kindness and respect will pay dividends: an outcome that Terri proves in *The Champagne CEO,* and one that I've borne witness to over the past thirty-plus years of our professional and social relationship.

I first met Terri when I was at Time Inc., launching *InStyle* magazine in June of 1993. One of Terri's brands was on our target list for advertising partnerships. So, while it was (and is) *de rigueur* to get vague parameters or incomplete information when attempting to pitch advertisers, it was not so with Terri Eagle on the other side of the phone. She gave us exactly what we needed to tailor our pitch to win her business, and she was a steadfast partner from then on, always providing useful (if sometimes brutally direct) feedback. You always know where you stand with her—one of her superpowers is being honest and direct with colleagues and business partners, and it always serves both parties well ... even when it's tough to hear.

Over the years I've come to know Terri as an effective leader and cheerleader for the causes and partners in which she believes, and that drive to win is incredibly contagious. Her quick ability to assess a situation, make a decision, and move her company forward makes her an exceptional leader. It also makes Terri an exceptional friend. Her attention to detail in everything from gifts to thoughtful additions to a dinner party hints at a holistic philosophy to entertaining that encompasses a straightforward warmth full of surprise and delight.

This duality of "down-to-business happy warrior executive" and "hyper-engaged practitioner of joy" is precisely what you should expect from this book: that you can be a great (empathetic, firm, even-handed) leader, but always treat people with respect. And I think that it's something we can all aspire to in work, life, and self.

INTRODUCTION

Have you ever woken up in the morning fresh and eager to start the new day, only to have a roadblock come your way several hours later? It might be a business-related issue that you know will take a long time to work out. Or it could be a challenge you're facing in your personal life. Whatever it is, it has the potential to divert your day or, at the very least, cause you to feel disappointed about what's ahead.

I'm here to say (and I've lived it!) that in those moments, you have a choice to make. You can choose to smile and work to solve the problem, or you can decide to frown and give up. In my case, I really try to smile. I love to bring enthusiasm to everyone around me, in all situations, both the good and the challenging. Even if there are steep barriers in the way at work or personally, I like to smile first. With good energy and a happy tone, I then work through what's in the way.

It may mean making phone calls, setting up a meeting, changing my schedule, or even taking the day to do something else than I originally planned. It's my aim to always keep going. I find that there's always something to celebrate—and I love to focus on the joys of life and business. It's what makes the small moments matter and how each day can have a sparkle of its own. It's why I am known as the Champagne CEO and how you can be too.

While this may sound trivial, I can assure you it's not a flaky take on how to live—not at all. Rather, it's a heartfelt way to approach both business and life. Trust me, I know what it's like to get through hard times! But I also know how great it feels to win. I've always had a great desire to achieve and accomplish every goal I take on. And I've won—many times.

I've reinvented myself five different times in five different industries. I've worked my way up the ladder, from selling Camp Fire Girl cookies at age nine to being a salesgirl at a pharmacy's makeup department and eventually holding senior-level executive positions. I recently was president and CEO at Morilee, a leading bridal and special occasion designer, manufacturer, and wholesaler that operates globally and sells to more than sixty countries.

I've spent the last twenty-five years of my career leading luxury brands to profitable growth in the retail industry (sometimes through astronomic gains!). I've built a track record along the way, and companies count on me to create strategies, build brands, plan for the long term, develop the business, and ultimately deliver, time and again.

This idea of smiling and having the right attitude, coupled with a focus on relationships, has brought me to where I am today. I've built relationships in business on many levels. I've met with owners of privately held businesses, executive management of premier global department stores, and CEOs of international brands, discussing and negotiating new business growth opportunities.

I've built up successful teams, and I continually look for ways to empower and encourage my employees. It's important to me to make others feel good and for it to go well for them. If you work for me, for instance, you can expect to get a gift box every time it's your birthday. I also love the element of surprise, and I've been known to order champagne for my staff while they're on vacation and hand out special gifts to guests at my dinner parties. I think these extra touches can help others know they are appreciated.

That's not to say I haven't had some hard knocks throughout my career, and I'll share these in the pages that follow. I invite you to see this book as a chance to sit down together, to go over stories that you can absorb, and then apply their takeaways to your own life. I'll share the path that I took to get to where I am today and how each situation was a chance to grow and build in some way.

You'll find there are five parts to the book, and each one focuses on a different capability that can help you achieve success both in your career and in your life. The first part covers the idea of believing in yourself, even if you don't have an extensive support system. In the parts that follow, we'll look at the importance of asking for what you'd like to achieve, taking risks, and learning from each experience you have. Finally, I'll touch on the essential component of care, both in the sense of looking after your teams and relationships and also prioritizing balance and your own well-being.

After reading this book, you'll be equipped every day to wake up and have a new lease on life. You'll see each morning as a fresh start and chance to improve on what you've already accomplished, to try new things, to be brave, and to take risks. You'll want to nurture the relationships in your life and remember that people really make all the difference. You'll be able to show that you care, both at work and in your personal life, and can reap the benefits that come from doing so. Most of all, you'll be inspired to have fun in both your professional and personal life. You'll want to toast along with me to a fabulous career and the joys that are waiting for us tomorrow.

One last note before we begin: the pillars of smiling and focusing on relationships that I mentioned were not my own inventions. I owe those teachings to my father, who showed me through his example and the conversations we had about how to be kind, how to treat others, and how to work hard. As you read on, you'll learn more about the impact he had on me, my life, and my career.

For now, I want you to know that Dad would want me to always smile. That was his wish, and that's what I do today. I hope that after reading this book, you'll do the same.

PART ONE

BELIEVE

CHAPTER ONE

A PRICELESS FOUNDATION

After owning and operating a pizza franchise called Pizza Pete, my dad went on a new venture. He sold the chain, cashed out life insurance policies, and together with my mom opened an Italian restaurant in a suburb of Seattle in his midforties. He started the venture with my stepmom, who had an Italian background. The menu was family-style and delicious, and the menu included pizza that was based on a recipe he had spent years refining.

For the first three weeks of business, the place was empty. Seeing that no one was coming in, Dad decided to try something else. He ran some ads, even though funds for the place were tight at the time. In fact, my parents had borrowed money from my grandparents to buy the restaurant. There was a lot of risk riding on the eatery. No one could guarantee it would generate an income, let alone enough to live on.

As it turned out, Dad's marketing efforts were successful. People came, and the place buzzed with activity. Dad was able to pay off the loan he had taken from my grandparents in the first year of the pizza business. He and my stepmom ran it for the following twenty years. Eventually, he sold it to his manager when he was sixty years old on a ten-year personal loan to the manager.

I had some of my first lessons in business with Dad at Pizza Pete, the franchise he owned and operated prior to starting the Italian restaurant Aversano's. He was involved with Pizza Pete about fifteen years before opening the new restaurant. I started working there when I was fifteen years old. By then, I had already done some other jobs and discovered what it was like to work toward accomplishing goals. In every setting, Dad taught me so much, and his teaching expanded beyond the restaurant. He showed me what it meant to work hard to find time for people in your life and to always be kind to everyone.

The Value of Hard Work

My parents divorced when I was just seven years old, which was not very common in my area at that time. Both went on to remarry and live different lives, and I loved the two sets of parents I had in my life. My stepfather was a Renaissance man and very successful in what he did. Dad worked so hard, and he instilled in me the importance of going after a goal, even when it's challenging.

Drawing on these examples, I started working at an early age. And when I took on something, I always wanted to do my best and get the prize. I loved winning. My first business experience involved selling Camp Fire Girl mints in my neighborhood. They tasted pretty great, and I learned I could run faster than any of the girls in the neighborhood. I sold the most cookies of everyone! I did this starting at age ten and continued until I was twelve years old. I loved getting the badges and honors that followed those sales.

When I was about ten years old, my mom sent me and my sister to the strawberry fields during the summer to work. We would get on a bus and take it to the strawberry farm, where we would pick berries and get money for the baskets that we filled. I did that for two summers, and then I started looking for something else.

At age twelve, I decided to start a babysitting business that I ran on my bike. I would ride around the neighborhood and book appointments with anyone who needed help. In addition to babysitting, I was soon asked to do other odd jobs like ironing. Business went so well that I booked gigs from morning to night and even worked weekends all summer long. My parents opened a savings account for me, and I had to put half of my earnings into the account. Even with setting aside much of my pay, I made enough to get some fun purchases for myself.

FINDING TIME FOR RELATIONSHIPS

My parents, and especially Dad, worked long hours and had to oversee detailed operations with very few breaks. Despite the commitment he had to the restaurant to keep it running and make sure it was profitable, he always made time for his family. He consistently would check to see that my sister and I were happy. He loved to sit and talk to us whenever he could.

During these times together, he never spoke a negative word. Instead, he would treat us well, and sometimes he would take me and my sister on adventures or to partake in fun activities together. He would often drive us to our grandparents' house, and I grew close to those relatives as a result. Dad also taught us to play miniature golf and to enjoy life's treats, like indulging in cotton candy.

BEING NICE TO EVERYONE

During my freshman year of high school, I decided that I wanted to be a cheerleader. When my dad first heard about my idea, he didn't want me to try out. Instead, he took me to Ocean Shores, a beach in Washington, and sat me down for a talk.

He started by explaining his reason for being against me being a part of the team. "The cheerleaders I knew," he began, "were not very nice." He paused and then continued, "Listen, honey, you can try out. I'll let you do it, because you'll probably make it on the squad. But you have to promise me that you'll always be nice to everyone in school. You will smile, and you'll be pleasant."

I did try out, and as Dad predicted, I made the cheerleading team. I was friends with other girls in the group, and I followed Dad's advice. I made sure I was nice to everyone and remained positive, even when practices were tough.

After I joined the team, Dad had more words to share with me. "Don't get into trouble," he said, "because I don't have time to deal with it. I work too hard." I followed this guidance as well.

Learning at the Restaurant

While I was in high school, and after I landed the cheerleading position, Dad let me have a job at one of the restaurants in his pizza chain, Pizza Pete. I was fifteen years old, and when summer rolled around, I lived with him for the summer months of break. I divided my time between cheerleading and working at the restaurant.

I was thrilled to have a job there, and I was ready to see what Dad would ask me to do. As it turned out, he had a system for new hires, much like a training program, to introduce staff members to the operations and customer service staff. At first, I worked in the table section. I greeted customers and showed them to their tables. Then I picked up dishes and took them to the back, where they would be washed. That lasted for about a month, and after that, I graduated to the cash register.

I was very excited to be able to count the money and did so at the beginning of my evening shift and also at night when the restaurant closed. The following month, I moved to the pizza counter and learned how to make the pies with just the right amount of ingredients. Dad always watched carefully to make sure that the correct portions were given, to keep the cost of goods from going too high.

I loved my time at the restaurant. It was fun to learn how to work, to be with Dad, and to watch my earnings. I had a bank account and a savings account, and I kept an eye on them as they increased. I knew then that business thrilled me, and I would follow that course for my long-term career.

SETTING THE STAGE FOR ACHIEVEMENT

Later in high school, I decided I wanted to be on the homecoming court. My dad wanted to see me achieve this goal too. There was one problem though. According to the school's government council, you couldn't be nominated to be on the court if you were a cheerleader. If I wanted to accomplish my goal of being part of the homecoming royalty, I would first have to change the school's policy.

So, following Dad's example of taking risks and pushing forward, I got on the government council. I worked with others to help change the policy and allow cheerleaders to get nominated. We were able to get a new rule in place that made it possible for cheerleaders to be on the homecoming court. When the time for the big event came, I was nominated and became one of the princesses on the court. It was a big win for me, and I couldn't wait to be on the float for the parade with the other royalty. Dad came to watch the float and the game for homecoming that year. He was so happy and proud of me and knew what I had done to get there. It became a special event for both of us.

One time, during high school, there was a contest to write a speech about our dads. Every entry was to have the title "Why My Dad Is Number One." Our writings were to reflect why we admired our fathers and what we appreciated about them. I decided to contribute and went up against the six hundred other students at the school. After we submitted the speeches, we were invited to come to an event where they would read the winning one.

The night of the contest final, I didn't know if Dad would be able to make it. He had broken his ankle while working at a restaurant he had just purchased. I went to the event with my sister, and we waited to see if Dad would arrive. Soon, we saw him come in on crutches. He had made it (I should have known—he always made it to our special events).

The audience quieted as the speaker prepared to read the winning speech. We listened intently along with the crowd. Then I heard the words that were being read, and I knew … it was the one I wrote about my dad. I had included how he always made time for us and encouraged us to follow our dreams. My writing had won—but really, Dad had won it for being the best dad he could be.

That speech really became the theme of my life in the years that followed. As I chased my career dreams, moved around the country, and went after positions of leadership, Dad was always beside and behind me. I called him once a week for years, and we regularly got together.

When he retired from the pizza business, Dad found new hobbies to enjoy, including a love for golf. He kept a vegetable garden and also took a liking to dahlias, which are beautiful and colorful perennials. His work ethic was still strong from his restaurant days, and he stayed active for many years. At one point, he planted five hundred dahlias in his front yard, and the result was gorgeous. He became such a master at gardening that his flowers won awards. He often participated in the Puyallup Fair in Washington, where his dahlia flowers won ribbons. (If he didn't get all first-place prizes at a fair, he was distraught!)

Even as I became very busy with my career (and I'll cover those experiences more in the coming chapters) and traveled frequently, I kept in touch with Dad. He was always eager for news from me. He continued to be a source of encouragement for me, and our relationship strengthened even more over the years.

When I visited his home and beautiful yard, I would always bring some Merlot wine for him. Merlot was his favorite. We would then sit together in his home in the Seattle area and sip a drink while we talked about life, his garden, work, and everything in between. He always wanted to know how my work was going, and he was a constant support for me. He would assure me he loved me and let me know that I would be able to make it through whatever challenges lay ahead.

Sadly, Dad passed away in October 2020 at age eighty-nine. And yet, part of him is still with me. He was such an important figure in my life and showed me how to work hard and to keep relationships in the forefront. To this day, I can still hear the way he ended our phone conversations by saying, "Honey, I love you, and I'm so proud of you."

Everything that I've accomplished stems from the upbringing I had and the role models in my life who set a path to follow. Dad instructed me to be kind to others (and not take on poor habits as a cheerleader!), and I try to do that every day, with everyone in my life. I don't take relationships for granted, and I value the people on my team.

In a way, this book is my way of sharing his message with you, dear reader. As you go through life, as you take on new positions and look to move up, I encourage you to look for opportunities, to make the leap, to work hard, and above all, to remember that people matter. Lead with heart, and you'll be able to achieve big wins in work and in life.

Key Takeaways

- Striving for a goal often requires hours of hard work, and it's not always clear how the end will turn out. If you go after the win and commit to making it work, your chances of success will increase.
- While working hard is a key component to getting ahead, it's also important to find those moments when you can step back, slow down, and be with the people you love.
- Even when it's tough, being kind to others provides the assurance that you're putting in the effort to present yourself well and gives others the opportunity to establish a relationship with you.
- Achieving goals like starting a restaurant or moving up in your career often comes with a future that is unknown. Believe that you can give it your best, and then get ready to see the results that follow.

CHAPTER TWO

THE LAUNCHPAD

I will forever be grateful for the first working experiences I had during my youth, from selling cookies in the neighborhood to serving customers at Pizza Pete. I learned something at every place, and collectively, they gave me a great foundation on which to build my career.

When I was sixteen years old in high school, I took on another job—this time at a local pharmacy. While I had enjoyed working with Dad, he lived an hour away from where I lived during the school year. The pizza restaurant was in his area of town too. It wasn't practical to stay there during the school year.

The pharmacy, however, was within walking distance of where I lived while I went to high school. I applied there, thinking it would be a great opportunity to be part of a company. It was really fancy inside, with a section for gifts and cosmetics, along with other departments you wouldn't expect to see in a typical drugstore.

After I was hired, I began working at the cashier counter. Then I received training for the other departments. After about six months, I started working in the cosmetics section. I soon fell in love there. The products felt so special, and I got such a thrill selling to people and making them happy. As a young person, working in this area was like a dream; in fact, I thought I had made it big time!

Of course, due to the limits placed on the number of hours that young people can work, together with my other responsibilities as a cheerleader, I was only at the pharmacy for about twenty hours a week. My schedule usually included working at the store on the weekends and a couple of nights each week. Still, these time slots allowed me the chance to interact with customers, learn more about cosmetics and the different brands that sold them, and observe other sales professionals who were willing to share their knowledge and offer further training. Ultimately, my experience at that pharmacy would become a launchpad that helped me jump into my full-time career in sales and marketing and take on leadership roles along the way.

Meeting Sales Reps

During my time working at the pharmacy, I noticed that on occasion, different sales reps would come in and visit the store. They would make connections and evaluate how their products were performing. They would check on inventory, and I would help them fill in orders. I was fascinated by these visitors, as they were always dressed so well and looked professional.

One in particular, Jenefer Lass from L'Oréal, looked exactly like someone I wanted to be. She was poised, smart, and dressed fabulously. I noticed her British accent right away and also saw that she wore simple and elegant jewelry. She was a sales manager at L'Oréal and represented the brand well. I thought L'Oréal stood above the other product lines in terms of quality and presentation. I remember thinking, "It would be great to have a job there."

In addition to seeing sales reps in the pharmacy, I was given the chance to attend training sessions hosted by different companies like Revlon, L'Oréal, Coty, and Physicians Formula, which were often held at really nice hotels in the area. I would go for a half or full day, depending on the brand. During these sessions, I would get information related to a new color scheme or an up-and-coming fragrance story. The instructors would also teach us how to sell their brand's products. They showed how to ask open-ended questions and lead into the sale.

Again here, I noticed that L'Oréal's training was top-of-the-line. I learned how to layer products and sell other items that complemented what the customer was interested in. For instance, if someone was buying a fragrance, we were taught to recommend getting the soap and lotion with the same scent to go with it. That way, it would last a longer time. The training classes left a distinct impression on me. I thought I had the coolest job in the world.

Landing a New Position

I stayed at the pharmacy and continued working during the rest of my high school years. After some time, the company was purchased by another one called Shoppers Drug Mart. As one of Canada's largest retailers, based in Toronto, Ontario, it was going through a period of expansion.

After I graduated from high school and was on my way to college, I was offered the role of cosmetics manager. I was excited and eagerly accepted the position. Then, after Shoppers Drug Mart had acquired the pharmacy, the brand went on to buy other stores in the area. They soon gave me a new offer too. They asked if I would be the coordinator of five stores they had purchased in the vicinity. I was eighteen years old at the time, and I continued working even as college started. I attended a university in the area and put myself through school.

I loved the new role and looked for ways to be creative. I would coordinate events to drive sales and bring in customers. For example, I asked sales representatives from the different brands we worked with to come and give free makeovers. This way, customers could try out the products, see which ones worked, and buy the ones they liked.

Even as I worked with different cosmetic brands, I kept thinking that getting more involved with L'Oréal would be a great opportunity. Soon, I had set my sights on a new goal. I wanted to be a sales representative for L'Oréal, and I started looking for ways to get the position. Since I had met Jenefer Lass and was impressed by her, I asked her for the chance to work as a sales representative. I had finished college by this point.

She told me, "Oh, Terri, you don't have outside sales experience." She was making the point that while I was working at the cosmetic counter, it was a relatively safe environment. Customers came to me, not the other way around. I would have to go out and prove myself if I wanted the job.

At first, I was a little put out. After all, I had been working hard since I was a youth! I had realized that I could sell to people, and I had a skill set to communicate well and tell a story. Moreover, I was ready to move up in my career and saw the company as a great way to do this. It was frustrating to know I was not considered to be a L'Oréal sales rep … yet!

FINDING A PATH FORWARD

After thinking about it, I took Jenefer's words to heart and brainstormed different ways to build up some experience. I soon came across an ad in the newspaper that stated Russ Berrie and Company was hiring. The company was looking for a sales representative for the state of Washington. Named after its founder, Mr. Russell Berrie, the company specialized in designing and selling stuffed animals, toys, and gifts. For many years, it was well known for the teddy bears it made and was one of the world's largest gift companies.[1]

Mr. Berrie was a master marketer of toys and an incredibly generous businessman. After growing up in the East Bronx and becoming a salesman for a toy company, he identified an opportunity in the market for inexpensive gifts and stuffed animals that shoppers might see displayed on a shelf or near the checkout line in a store. He brought the idea up to his boss, who passed on it, so Mr. Berrie started on his own in a rented garage space in 1963.[2] The company grew quickly, and by 1966, its annual sales revenue exceeded $1 million. Much of its success was due to Mr. Berrie's ideas for toys and gifts, together with his ability to understand people and make a sale.[3]

To apply for the position at Russ Berrie and Company, we were asked to come to an open-interview hiring event at 9:00 a.m. on an appointed day at the Marriott hotel near Sea-Tac, a Seattle Southside

---

1 Eric Pace, "Russell Berrie, 69, Founder of a Toy and Gift Company, Has Died," *New York Times*, December 27, 2002, https://www.nytimes.com/2002/12/27/business/russell-berrie-69-founder-of-a-toy-and-gift-company.html.

2 "About Russ Berrie," Russell Berrie Foundation, accessed April 19, 2024, https://www.russellberriefoundation.org/our-founder.

3 Pace, "Russell Berrie."

suburb. Sea-Tac is centered around the Pacific Northwest's largest international airport.[4]

The interview event was to take place in the ballroom at the Marriott Sea-Tac hotel, and I knew it would be great! After thinking about it, I decided to attend and apply. It would be a chance to gain more outside experience as Jenefer had suggested. I picked out my outfit for the day, which included a ladies' suit and skirt, blazer, blouse, and heels. It was very much a Jenefer Lass look. When I walked in, I quickly realized the interview process was not going to be a typical conversation with an executive to see if I was a good fit and then going home to wait for a phone call letting me know if I had been hired. Instead, when I entered the ballroom, I saw there were over two hundred people in it. At the stage in the center of the ballroom stood Mr. Russ Berrie himself. He would be carrying out the interview and selection process. Out of everyone in attendance, just one person would get the position.

The setup was almost like a sell-off to see who would win the sales rep position. One by one, each of us walked up to the stage where Mr. Berrie stood. We each were given a Montblanc motif pen, and we were told that we should sell it to him. We had three minutes for our turn, and after we tried to get the sale, we would be told if we were rejected or if we could continue to the next round. Those who were rejected had to leave the ballroom; those who stayed would advance to the next round. The cycle would continue until only one contestant remained.

When it was my turn, I walked onto the stage, and Mr. Berrie handed me a Montblanc motif pen. "Sell me this," he said.

I was nervous, but I knew what to say. After all, I had attended the cosmetics classes and had learned the language to use. I knew how

4 "SeaTac," Visit the USA, accessed April 19, 2024, https://www.visittheusa.co.uk/destination/seatac.

to professionally sell, and I put my skills to work during those few minutes. I was friendly to Mr. Berrie and asked open-ended questions so that I couldn't get a "no" response.

When my three minutes were up for that first round, I waited to see what would happen next. Would I be rejected and asked to leave? Or would I be able to stay?

To my excitement, I advanced to the next round. And the next. And the next. After five rounds with Mr. Berrie, I made the final pick. I had gotten the job, and I was just twenty-three years old!

It was a big win for me. I felt truly honored that I had the chance to talk to Mr. Berrie, a great salesman and businessman himself, and that he had given me the chance to be a sales representative in his company. The position would pay based on commission, and I would get 10 percent of the sales.

What did Mr. Berrie see in me? Perhaps he realized I had been trained to ask the right questions. I was also pleasant, as I continued to live by my father's guidance to be nice to everyone. Perhaps he thought I was really engaging, and I was certainly young and excited about the job. On top of that, I had dressed really well, based on what I had observed other sales reps, including Jenefer, wear. It was a thrill to have such a successful person pick me from among the other two hundred contestants for the job.

While there certainly was an element of luck as well, like there always is in sales, I thought the experience came full circle later when I took on a sales leadership role at Montblanc, of all places! After landing a job by trying to sell their pen, I went to work for them. I'll share more of that story in a later chapter.

When I was hired by Russ Berrie and Company, I saw a path in my mind of how to move forward. I could work hard in sales at the company and gain valuable experience. I would put in extra effort, following the example of Dad and the dedication he had shown to me. I knew he would be proud of me for getting the position and excited about what lay ahead for me and my career. If all went well with the toy company, I would be able to go back to Jenefer and show that I had made sales in other areas. That could convince her to hire me for the job I wanted at L'Oréal.

Getting Ready to Launch

Once I started at Russ Berrie and Company, I was practically in flight mode. My career was taking off, and I used my time at the company as a way to spring into the next position. I'll share more of that story in the next chapter (stay tuned!).

For now, it's a good time to pause and think about ways to get those opportunities to launch. When I was looking for a job and applying at Russ Berrie and Company, it was not easy. It can be tough to find doors that will open (especially when the ones we want are closed, which was the case for me when I initially asked to work at L'Oréal).

That's why when people come to me now, after seeing the track record I've established, and ask me for advice on the job search, I always invite them to see it as a full-time business. By that, I mean you have the option of treating the process as if it's your job. It could take up eight hours (or more!) of your day, every day.

It's also important to make good use of that time. While you can certainly use job search tools online and connect with people on LinkedIn, I always encourage others to find face-to-face opportunities as well. I also advise others to become like an octopus. Get your fingers out there and think, "Who do I know?" Sit down and make a list of everyone that might give you a job lead or helpful career insight. Then start working your way through the names.

You can reach out to others in your circles who might have some insight to share and invite them out for a coffee and a chat. Just remember to be respectful of their time and to be pleasant when you make a request. Those with experience and expertise are often willing to share their knowledge with someone who is looking to launch, especially if that person comes across as motivated and eager to learn.

I also suggest doing informational interviews, which are conversations you can have with a professional to talk about your job opportunities. They might be involved in an industry you want to enter, or they could have insight into a company you're hoping will hire you. These discussions may also focus on general career advice, such as what questions to expect in an interview, how to answer, ways to stand out among other candidates, and how to get a promotion. These are usually best held with someone who has had a successful career and loves to mentor others.

Not long ago, I helped line up informational interviews for my best friend Lael's son, Ethan. I knew he had attended Vanderbilt University and played baseball while there. He had done very well and became recognized for his baseball skills. Ethan was the starting second baseman and team leader on Vanderbilt's College World Series winning team. Out of college, he was drafted by the Pittsburgh Pirates, and then, after giving his next steps some thought, he returned to Vanderbilt and earned an MBA through a two-year program that was available to him.

As his graduation approached, I decided to reach out. His journey through college and beyond showed that he had some remarkable training and skills. However, I also was aware that while he had ample experience playing baseball, he didn't yet have a background in business. He also wasn't sure of what direction he wanted to take. In addition to finding a path forward and a way to launch his career, he would need to help others see that he could apply his past experiences to the new role. He was a team player and was known by his team and coaches as having confidence and being an outstanding communicator. He had learned to get through challenges, which could aid him as he started a new job.

When I spoke to Ethan and offered to introduce him to some in my circle that I respected, he readily agreed. I went ahead and made the connections, and Ethan was able to speak to people who were in leadership and executive positions. They all coached him on his job possibilities and the interview process. They helped him prepare for tough questions he would likely be asked. After these conversations, he was ready to move ahead. He found an opportunity for a managerial role at Vanderbilt and applied. And he got the job! It was set to begin in July 2024 with people-reporting responsibilities.

When I sit back and think about my time at the pharmacy, I have to smile. I always recall how I got such a thrill working at the cosmetics counter, and I'm grateful for the interaction I had with professional sales reps. Thanks to the time they spent with me and what they taught me, I was able to make a good impression on Mr. Berrie and get a job to launch my career. We'll look at what happened while I was with Russ Berrie and Company in the next chapter.

For now, know that if you're looking for a job, keep asking! Work like an octopus and tap the sources you can in order to get the information and skills you need. If you stay dedicated to the job search, you can find a way to launch your own path forward too.

Key Takeaways

- The foundation for a great career can often be tracked to early jobs and experiences. Whether it's selling cookies, working at a pharmacy, or doing something else, you can typically learn some skills and knowledge that can be applied to your next roles.
- While I was at the pharmacy, I realized I really loved the sales process. Once you find your passion, it might make the workload seem easier.
- Role models can teach us so many lessons and taking note of what they do could be a first step to launching your own career.
- To find your path forward, reach out to others and look for ways to connect face-to-face when possible. Ask questions, be ready to listen, and apply their insight to your job search to help you land the perfect-for-you position.

CHAPTER THREE

FIRST CHANCES

Shortly after Mr. Berrie hired me for his company, I had a huge bag of toys sent to my house. The package was filled with stuffed animals, and they were as cute as could be. I knew it was time to get to work helping others to see, as I did, just how special they were. I was ready to prove to Jenefer that I could get outside sales experience and do well so she would want to hire me.

I soon realized I would need to have a strategy to cover the entire state of Washington. I had a great car, as I've always loved driving around a nice vehicle, and I would be paying all my expenses, including gas and meals, while I traveled. I would need to make sure the commission covered these costs and more so that I could have a salary. In addition, I would have to be creative and think of a way to get those toys on store shelves.

Fortunately, I knew I had a lot going for me already. My father had established a solid foundation that I could build on, and I could strike up a friendly conversation with anyone. I have always enjoyed keeping notes and following schedules, and I love to find ways to engage with people. Washington State was about to find a new sales representative in its towns, with a bag full of toys and a fun story to share.

Working Off a Plan

To get started as a sales representative for Russ Berrie and Company, I was given a file that had some existing accounts. There weren't too many of them, and none of them had made significant orders or sent in regular payments for an extended period. While this meant there wasn't much to work with at first, it also showed that there was ample room for growth—if I could come up with an effective sales strategy.

I had never been in a position where I was so much on my own before, so I knew I had to create a plan. I pulled out a map and looked over the state. I wanted to follow up on the existing accounts and see if those retailers were interested in paying their balances and ordering more toys. I also had to find new locations. I pulled out the Yellow Pages to find listings of stores in different cities. It was important to me to do research so that I could make the most of my trips and stops. If I went about it haphazardly, I would risk not being prepared, making a mistake, and ultimately not getting a sale.

I used a paper planner to map out my routes and list what I would do in each place. To get ready for a trip, I would load up the bag of cute little stuffed animals—it was nearly bigger than me!—and say to them, "Here we go again!" They traveled with me in the car to different towns and places.

Once I arrived at the destination, I would get out and walk around to take in the area. I liked to bring the stuffed animals along with me into the stores, where I would pull them out and interact with them. One of the theories that Mr. Berrie had about selling the merchandise was that a gift could make someone feel good. I knew it would be helpful for the people in charge of the orders to see these toys in person. It would help them understand how their customers might want to buy them as gifts for someone in their life. Given this, I took the stuffed animals out of the bag and put them on the counter of every store I entered. Then I played with the toys. Often the owners would join in and play too!

I would always talk about the prices as well. When Mr. Berrie started the company, his idea was to sell a toy for just one dollar and make gifts that could be like a card. Rather than giving a person a piece of paper, you could give a gift of a stuffed animal, often with a cute message on it like, "I love you," or "My First Teddy."

While during the years that followed the start of the company, prices went up, the toys were still quite inexpensive for customers to buy. There was a price range for the different stuffed animals and gifts, and I would mention this when I visited retail shops. I would also share that the product lines were doing really well and then suggest that the store start with a smaller order, such as a dozen pieces.

When a retailer wanted to make an order, I would get out paper forms and fill them in by hand. It was exciting to sign up new accounts, and I kept careful records of the accounts and orders. I also noted appointments in my planner and tracked my costs too. It was important for me to document everything and follow my plan.

CREATING EXCLUSIVITY

During the weeks that followed, I taught myself how to cover the sales region I was assigned. Yet I also knew that if I sold the stuffed animals to every single store in a town, the area would be saturated, and it might be hard for retailers to sell their merchandise. The supply might be more than the demand, which could be detrimental for future orders. Also, the toys might not be perceived as something unique if customers could see them and get them anywhere. I had to come up with a distribution plan to make everybody feel special.

With that in mind, I decided to pick the locations where I would showcase the stuffed animals. If the city had a hospital, I always chose the gift shop in the hospital. Since the merchandise was designed to be a special gift, I thought they could have real meaning and purpose by being on the shelves. Visitors could get them for their loved ones who had an operation, were undergoing treatment, or simply needed a pick-me-up. They could also be purchased for children coming to the hospital to visit their loved ones or going home after seeing a patient.

In addition, I would choose another store, such as a nice flower store or gift shop, in the town. When I went into these places, I would mention that I was only going to sell the toys in two locations. This helped the person authorizing the order to see that there could be a demand for these items. It also created a sense of exclusivity, as it showed I was carefully selecting what I thought were the best locations for these toys.

Fast Growth

I worked tirelessly during the days that followed, spending months taking the toys on the road and selling them to hospital gift shops, flower shops, and other gift stores in the towns throughout the state. I opened new accounts and checked on existing ones. I was determined to take a good report to Jenefer after I had spent some time in sales on the road selling and opening new accounts.

After six months on the road and with the job, I learned incredible news. At the California national sales meeting, there was an award given for the sales representative with the highest percentage of increased sales during the previous six months. Based on what I had sold in Washington, I won the prize! I was so happy to have that accomplishment. I knew Dad would be proud too.

Crafting a Sales Pitch

If you want to make it as a salesperson or help others to buy into your idea, the approach you take will play an important part. You'll want to think about what you're going to say and how you'll say it. I still remember what I would share when I walked into those stores throughout Washington. It went something like this:

"Hello, I'm Terri, and I'm the representative for Russ Berrie, and I would love to share this collection with you. I'm only going to sell these toys in two locations: your place and the hospital. And I always come to my favorite first, and I would love to sell these here for you. I have a wide range of prices, and you know, the line is doing really well ..." After we had chatted and played with the toys and I could see their interest, I would often close the sale by saying, "Why don't we start with twelve pieces for your store?"

Notice the friendly, casual tone, and the fun engagement along the way. While I would ask questions and get to know the people in the shops, I would also show that their store could be selling a special collection and join in the chance to be part of a trend that was going well. I would avoid talking too much and instead give the other person the opportunity to talk about what was on their mind. If I knew the challenges they faced, I might be able to help them find a solution. Plus, people tend to enjoy the opportunity to open up and share.

I still love to sell, to get to know people, to be creative, and to have fun. Importantly, I also believe in being prepared and having a plan. Practice what you'll say in a pitch and think about how it will come across to others. Keep it short, and make sure it provides a solution for the client. Let them know your care, ask questions, and listen to their answers. The client might feel so comfortable with you and so appreciate the chance to be heard that they look to you when they need to make a purchase.

Doing Business with Kind People

How did I make so many sales during such a short time? Had I uncovered an incredible market or opportunity? That may have been part of it, and as I've mentioned, there's usually an element of luck too. That said, when I reflect on that time driving around the state of Washington with stuffed animals in my car, trying to make a sale at different stores, I think that the managers and owners I interacted with probably appreciated doing business with me.

At every stop, I worked to get to know the people I met. I built up strong relationships, and people could tell I really loved the stuffed animals I had with me.

I really believe that, at the end of the day, people like to do business with nice people. If you are pleasant, thoughtful, and show real interest in them and their business, people notice.

After a series of jobs during my schooling years, being a Russ Berrie and Company sales representative was my first chance to get outside experience. And I loved it. After I received the award, I also knew what I wanted to do next. I would go back to Jenefer and see if the position at L'Oréal was still open. If it was, I was hoping she would offer it to me. I was ready to move on, to move up, and to take on new challenges.

That's exactly what I did. I'll share the next legs of my sales journey and interactions with Jenefer in the following chapter. As this story closes, I want to emphasize the importance of taking opportunities seriously. They are often a chance to work hard and prove that we can get the job done. You might have to be creative to find a solution. But the win that comes after putting in your best effort is hard to beat!

I encourage you to identify the prize you want, create a plan and follow it, and watch the story unfold. You'll soon be on your way to telling stories about how you achieved a successful career too.

Key Takeaways

- Having a plan and a strategy can help you schedule your days. If you keep careful records, you'll have a way to track progress and evaluate what methods work well.
- If you can create a sense of exclusivity, buyers often love to be a part of it. Just be sure to do your research so you can reach out to the right places.
- People can often tell if you believe in a product and enjoy what you're doing. When selling, a casual, friendly approach can often lead to a positive outcome.
- Building rapport and showing kindness to others will enable you to build great relationships and could lead to long-term clients.
- Listen to others! Master your listening skills for better communication.

PART TWO

ASK

CHAPTER FOUR

EYE ON THE PRIZE

Working at Russ Berrie and Company gave me exactly what I needed to apply at L'Oréal. After I won the award for selling so many toys and stuffed animals, I called up Jenefer. She was still the sales manager at L'Oréal, and she remembered me.

After explaining my situation, I said, "If you still haven't filled that opening, can we meet?"

She explained that the position was still open. She also agreed to see me, and we set a time to have an interview. Jenefer suggested meeting at the Four Seasons hotel in Seattle. It was important to me to put my best foot forward, and that included choosing an appropriate outfit. When the day came, I showed up to the hotel in an elegant suit, skirt, and high heels. I was a great Nordstrom customer!

Walking in to the Four Seasons, I was glad I had chosen my attire well! It was one of the nicest hotels I had ever been. After Jenefer and I exchanged greetings, we spent some time going over my experience selling Russ Berrie merchandise around the state of Washington. I told her how I had set up my distribution plan, complete with choosing about two shops per town and creating a sense of exclusivity. I mentioned how I enjoyed the process and had played with the toys while interacting with clients too. Of course, I had to share my sales meeting award I had just won for the highest percentage of increased sales during the last six months!

Apparently, the experience I had at Russ Berrie and Company, along with my persistence in reaching out to her again, helped Jenefer see I was serious about getting into sales and taking on more responsibility. She still hadn't filled the position. At the end of our meeting together, she told me I was hired! I had gotten the job I was really hoping to have. I would be account executive in the Washington State and Alaska territory for L'Oréal. I received a company car, salary, commission, and special benefits.

While I knew that my hard work in the past jobs had helped to open this door, I would soon see that there was much to learn. Fortunately, Jenefer proved to be an exceptional mentor, and she dedicated time to training me. She showed me what to do to have a successful start at L'Oréal and taught me many skills that I still use today.

Learning from the Best

When Jenefer hired me, she was a national sales manager at L'Oréal, and she reported to the VP of sales in New York. She was also about twenty years older than me. I marveled at her experience and background. She had worked her way up the sales ladder over the years and held positions in other companies like Revlon. She had cut her teeth in a very hard environment and had learned to hold her own in tough business settings. As a female executive, I'm sure it wasn't easy for her to move into leadership positions.

Still, Jenefer had managed to take on roles with more responsibility, and she was eager to teach me how to do it too. As I got to know her, I was so impressed by how put together she always looked in a natural way. She always dressed for the occasion, and she loved to be active. She traveled frequently and played tennis regularly too. Just by observing her, I felt I wanted to be like her. She exuded success, leadership, and a caring attitude for everyone around her.

In her personal life, Jenefer had lost her husband, and that must have been very difficult for her. Perhaps as a way to cope, she dove into her work and kept going. She was passionate about her career and wanted to see me grow too. She likely noticed I was hardworking and eager to learn all I could to make it on my own too.

After she hired me, Jenefer spent considerable time showing me what I would be doing in my new role. I would be covering the territories of Washington and Alaska. There were one-hundred-plus accounts in all, including drugstore chains and department store accounts. It would require careful preparation and a plan to manage them all.

Public Speaking Tools

To get ready to carry out my new role, Jenefer arranged for me to take public speaking courses and selling and negotiation skills training. It was part of L'Oréal's training program, and it took about six months to complete. The idea was that I, along with other new hires, would learn to carry myself professionally when meeting with retailers. The company wanted us to practice what we would say, what questions we would ask, and how we would be making a sale.

For part of this training, the company brought in a videographer. As new hires, we prepared our pitch and then gave it to the camera.

After, we had to watch our tapes. It helped us to see what we were doing well and where we could improve. I soon realized there was so much to learn about the way we conducted ourselves as sales representatives, from the hand gestures we used to the tone of voice we conveyed and the questions we asked.

We also had role-playing sessions, in which we tried to sell to others on our team. Jenefer saw this interaction as highly important, since it gave us a chance to try out different techniques within the safety of our group. We could then talk about what worked and what could be changed. By watching others, we also had the chance to pick up on new strategies that we could apply to our own sales calls.

I had always found it easy to engage with people and sell—after all, I loved the whole process and had realized it was my passion by then. Plus, I was eager to learn as much as I could, put it to use, and move up. After the initial public speaking sessions ended, I felt ready to take the next step, which would include going with Jenefer to meet the different clients at the retail stores in my region.

Time Management Skills

In my role at L'Oréal, I would need to figure out how to cover the territory I had, which was much more extensive than my previous sales job. I would be making up a schedule and following it. It would be up to me to engage with the retailers who had accounts, to take on new orders, and to work to make more sales. This meant finding department stores, independent pharmacies, national drug chain accounts, and all locations that carried L'Oréal cosmetics, fragrances, and skin care.

Again, here, Jenefer came up with a plan to help me navigate the area. She called it "Work Week with Jenefer," and it consisted of her traveling around with me to the different places with L'Oréal accounts. Jenefer lived in Los Angeles at the time, and she came to Seattle to spend an entire week with me.

We arranged that I would pick her up in my car, ready to travel to different retailers during the day. To prepare for the outing, she told me to organize the information I had about the different clients. I was to prepare a file folder on every account. She also sent over an itinerary that I had to fill out before she arrived.

I followed Jenefer's instructions and got ready for our work week together to begin. The first morning, I picked her up from the hotel she was staying at, the Four Seasons Seattle, and we set off. We were to follow the itinerary I had set up. For the next hours, I tried to drive to the locations I had selected. (Perhaps I should quickly note here that I am not the greatest with maps—also during those days, we didn't have access to the GPS that is part of everyday life now!) I had trouble figuring out where to go, and wouldn't you know it, by about 12:00 p.m., we were lost.

As you can imagine, this didn't go over very well with Jenefer. When she realized that I couldn't find my way, she turned to me and said, "Can you just pull over to the side of the road?"

"Of course, Jenefer," I replied.

I slowed down and veered off to the side. I stopped the car and turned to face her.

"I want you and I to cut our day short," she began. "You can take me back to the hotel. You'll go home, and I want you to spend the rest of the day looking at the maps. I want you to outline every turn you need to make on the outside of the file folder for our whole week's plan. That way, we won't ever get lost again, because when we do, that's a loss of time and money."

I sat and listened as she continued, "This is important. Our time is precious, and I'm spending all week with you. To make it work, we have to at least get to the store. There's another thing I want you to do tonight. You need to call all the stores that you're planning to visit and let them know we're coming."

We had been planning to do about three sales calls a day, so that meant I would be making fifteen calls later that day.

I assured her that I really wanted to make it work and that the job was important to me too. I then took her back to the hotel as she had requested. I went home and got out the maps. I noted all the routes we would be taking each day. I marked up the front of every file folder with directions on how to get to the place.

Then I started making phone calls. I chatted with the department managers and worked to build a relationship with them, starting with our first conversation. I knew Jenefer was a little chatty, and she sincerely wanted to know the people that we would be meeting with. After each call, I made additional notes in the folder so that we would have some information to review before our sales call with each department manager.

The rest of the week went much better! The next day, I picked up Jenefer as planned, and we went to the stores listed on the itinerary. It was much easier to find them with my notes, and Jenefer was happy with the research I had done. I appreciated having her along, as she could give me feedback after every sales call. She emphasized knowing and understanding the people. I would find out personal information as I met with managers and owners. Jenefer suggested learning about their families and when they had birthdays so we would know who we were doing business with. I followed this advice and built some great relationships.

The week ended well too. By the time Jenefer went home to Los Angeles, I had learned what a difference mapping out routes could make. I had seen how to plan out a week of sales calls, including how to set up appointments and keep notes of personal information. Jenefer had taught me that small things matter, such as taking cookies or a cake for a birthday. I felt ready to take on my region by following her guidelines, and I knew she would continue to check up on me during the following weeks and months.

Ongoing Mentoring

Jenefer organized other training sessions for me and the other account executives at L'Oréal, all of which helped us continue to build our skills and grow. She arranged meetings for us to learn about planning and making budgets, along with other workshops and mentoring meetings.

When I think about the tactics and strategies I use today in sales and business, I can't help but think of Jenefer. She served as such a role model for me, and I learned an incredible amount just by watching her at work. She also faithfully followed my career, even after I left L'Oréal and went to work for other companies. She would call me and see what I was doing, if I was happy with it, and if I was being taken care of. If I were going through a move, she counseled me on the transition and helped me handle the change.

As I look back, I realize that Jenefer guided me for decades by using a technique I call "the velvet hammer." She balanced having a good relationship with teaching key skills. Sometimes having a tough conversation was necessary, as it could result in lessons learned. (I'm mentioning this concept of the velvet hammer here to credit it to Jenefer, and I'll address it further in a later chapter.)

Even as she took me further under her wing, Jenefer kept her standards high. She had such a presence about her, and I always wanted to please her. If I got things right, she would be very happy. If things weren't right, I could always tell by the way she carried herself; it would be obvious that she wasn't pleased. And I couldn't blame her for that. After all, I loved the thrill of a win (I always had!), and Jenefer always went out to win too.

CONTINUING TO MOVE UP

When I reflect on my path and career, I see that others have stepped in at different times and guided me through situations. Some took note of my goals and saw what I was striving for and then helped to put me on a path to achieve what I wanted. One in particular who really brought the absolute best out of me came into my life after I had moved away from L'Oréal. I was working at Montblanc at the time as VP of sales and marketing, and this gentleman, Stanislas de Quercize, was the CEO.

After I was hired, he joined the company and relocated from Paris to the USA. He came with an incredible background, including being part of a very powerful jewelry and watch conglomerate on the luxury market. Montblanc at the time was starting to build itself as a luxury brand around the globe. (I'll share the story of how I got to Montblanc in a later chapter.)

After we met, Stanislas saw that I had my eye on the future and was envisioning new roles such as being a CEO of a company (which I later went on to be!). He sent me and other team members to an executive management school. We were each given high-level coaches who worked with us individually for a year. That was the most incredible investment in my career.

Under the arrangement, I had a journal, and I kept track of my interactions with peers and those who reported to me during each week. At our session, we would review my notes. I started to learn that I needed to find out what motivated each person on my team. I learned to be an incredible listener, to ask questions and then draw out of people what they respond to and then manage into that.

> At the executive management school, I learned that listening is key! By paying attention, you can find out what motivates each team member and then manage into that.

After that year of coaching, I could more easily see that what motivated one person might not motivate the next. Some people might look for a nice letter, while others will seek a bonus or would like some words of encouragement. Sports fans might find a baseball ticket for selling the most in a quarter to be highly enticing. Others will be more family oriented and might look for time off. By understanding what people want, you can set goals accordingly, and know that if they reach them, they'll be satisfied with the result.

One of the most meaningful phrases Stanislas taught me during our time together was, "Be cool." He often said this before we went into tough meetings where we knew the stakes would be high. The others in attendance would be coming in with steep demands. But he knew just how to stay relaxed, start a discussion, and work together to find a solution.

Stanislas and I were only on the same team for five years. After that, he was promoted and went back to France for the new position. I will never forget the way he helped me grow in my management skills, though. He was an incredible mentor who recognized my goals and supported them.

PASSING IT ON

I wouldn't be where I am today without the great mentors and role models, including Dad, Jenefer, and Stanislas, who have made such an impact on my life and career. In addition to being grateful for the time they spent with me, I now look for ways to help others. I have spent time mentoring young people and sharing what I have learned with them. I have also hired coaches to work with my teams. I have had professionals come in to teach about balance in life and work, self-confidence, and effective communication. These sessions have had positive results, with team members thanking me for the time they spent with coaches and demonstrating improvements in performance.

If you're new to a position and open to learning, it may be a perfect time to look for a mentor. I've even found in my career that I've learned something from everyone I've worked with. If you're continually evaluating the leadership of others, you too will be able to decide what you want to emulate and incorporate into your own repertoire. And once you do, you could find new opportunities to move up in your career.

Key Takeaways

- Persistence can pay off! If you have your eye on a career opportunity, look for ways to work toward getting it. Even if you aren't successful right away, you'll learn lessons you can apply to continue moving up.
- If you have a mentor, listen to their advice, and try out their suggestions. They could become lifelong friends and advocates who help you on your journey for years to come.
- To find a mentor, look within your own company or network as a starting point. You might be able to get an introduction through an acquaintance.
- Once you've achieved a level of success, there could be ways to give back, either by offering your time or resources. Others might look to you for words of advice and opportunities too.

CHAPTER FIVE

CAN I HAVE MORE?

Once I was onboarded at L'Oréal and working in my region, I had an invitation to attend the national sales meeting for the year. It would be held in New York City, and I had never been there. I can still remember riding in a yellow taxicab through the city on my way from the airport. It was nighttime, and upon seeing the lights of the skyline, I was in awe of every aspect, from culture, entertainment, and arts to fashion, plus so much more.

Yet suddenly, there I was, taking in the sights and sounds of one of the leading business centers of the world. I traveled on my own, and when the cab came through the Lincoln Tunnel, it was such a thrill. I thought, "I have to work here. I've got to be somebody someday in New York City. I'll need to figure out how to do that."

Besides forming a dream of wanting to live in New York City, I developed another goal during that trip. At the national sales meeting, I watched the top salesperson of the year win a spectacular award. The winner received a Rolex Tiffany watch, along with an engraved

Tiffany plaque and a sash that said "Account Executive of the Year." I thought, "I want that too."

The next year would be spent trying to get that award and learning many lessons along the way. I needed to have a new plan, one that would take me from the basics of managing a region of the country to earning an award that was offered to the top-performing regional salesperson. I was ready for a new mission, and I had the work ethic to strive for the goal.

The National Sales Meeting

I spent the next days at the sales meeting for the year, which was held at the Marriott hotel, an incredible location for a beautifully decorated event. And L'Oréal had done everything first-class for all of us in attendance that year. There were more than four hundred sales account executives and sales managers from across the US who were there alongside me. Since the company had a strong training program, there were many opportunities to attend marketing presentations and learn about new trends.

Some of the activities were so entertainment-driven and well put together that it was almost like being at a business carnival. I enjoyed the classes, the breaks that we could use to socialize and make connections, and the energy surrounding everything. I was twenty-five years old at the time and completely mesmerized by it all.

When it came to the final night, there was a special dinner held to celebrate the sales of the past year. I can still remember walking into the ballroom where it was to take place. The scene was just gorgeous. The tables had stunning displays, a band was playing, and there was a festive, party-like atmosphere. There was a section of round tables where we were seated for the meal. After that, it would be time to hand out the awards for the year.

On that night, for the grand finale, the most coveted award was presented. It was given to the sales account executive of the year, the person who best managed their territory. When it was announced, I watched as the saleswoman who won went up to the stage. She was presented with a sash, a Rolex watch, and a beautiful Tiffany engraved plaque.

I applauded, along with the audience, to acknowledge her hard work and dedication. The ceremony had such an impact on me as a young person. I thought, "What would it be like if I won that?" I knew immediately that I wanted to do my very best during the following year to capture that amazing award.

The next day, there was a breakfast served at the hotel for all the attendees of the meeting. Then we flew home, back to our respective territories and sales accounts. I went back to Seattle, ready to come up with a plan that would help me become the account executive of the year and walk onto the stage too.

Making Phone Calls

While I knew what I wanted—to get the award—I didn't know exactly what criteria was used to choose the winner. I also wasn't sure how to manage my territory in a way that would help me stand out among others at L'Oréal. I needed some guidance and was hoping to find answers to my questions.

I could have called Jenefer, my mentor and a role model at L'Oréal who had hired me and trained me for the position that covered Washington and Alaska. Rather than picking up the phone to speak to her, I started to think about others in the company. I knew that the person who was most involved with the award was the vice president of sales for L'Oréal. I figured he probably knew what was needed to get the prize. He was Jenefer's boss, and I knew that Jenefer, as one of the top sales managers at the company, reported to him.

Since I thought he was probably the one making the decisions for the awards, I decided to call him first. I'm sure he was a bit taken aback by my boldness, though he did take my call. He was polite and listened as I introduced myself.

I explained that I oversaw the northwestern territory and that I had been at the company for less than a year. Then I said, "I would really appreciate understanding how you set the goals and make the decision to award the account executive of the year and give them a prize which includes the Rolex watch."

There was a pause, and perhaps he was trying to decide how to respond. He recovered quickly, though, and went on to say, "Well, it's a series of things. It's not just the sales; it's also covering the stores and doing your reports." He mentioned the need to hit different targets for each of the three divisions, which were skin care, fragrance, and cosmetics. He added that good relationships mattered too and that they would be factored into the final decision for the award.

I appreciated his willingness to spend time getting a thorough answer ready for me. He soon called me with Jenefer on the line, too, and they shared great information. Jenefer seemed genuinely excited that I had a high goal and wanted to help as best she could.

I walked away from it thinking that I had a good grasp on what I needed to do. They shared goals to work toward and mentioned the importance of tracking everything. I would need to keep well documented records and send everything in to have a chance at the top prize.

I realized I had a long list of tasks to do. I had to manage about one-hundred-plus accounts in the territory, and this included department stores, local independent pharmacies, and large drug chains. I would need to travel and use my time carefully (no more getting lost!). I would also have to be creative and think of ways to go above and beyond what had been done in the past.

Finding New Opportunities

My trips to Alaska had to be well planned and maximized, due to the distance I was covering (and the high targets I was trying to achieve!). I would travel from Seattle to Anchorage and then rent a car to get around to the different places. Even though the climate was different, and my trips often involved getting through snow, I packed great-looking clothes. I always wore professional attire and fashionable heels. (Nordstrom all the way!)

It took some work to dress well in Alaska, as the temperatures sometimes reached thirty below zero, and the snow stacked up in high walls along the roads. I usually had to wear boots to get from one place to another. Still, I had seen Jenefer wear high heels, and I wanted to have a good presentation too. I kept my high heels in a separate bag that I carried around. Once I got inside a place, I would take off the boots and put on the heels. They went well with the suit jackets and skirts I had brought along for the different places.

As I drove around this northern state, I spoke with many people. I learned that oftentimes, the residents had limited shopping choices. These individuals lived on small islands off the mainland and came in by boat or a prop plane to the larger cities to shop. They might fly into Sitka, Anchorage, Fairbanks, or Juneau on occasion to stock up on supplies. Those were the four hubs of the state. Then they would go back to their residences in the remote areas.

This presented an untapped market in Alaska, and I found that if I went to the state and set up L'Oréal products in a place where they could be found, shoppers were eager to buy. I sold large amounts of cosmetics, skin care, and fragrances to these island dwellers. They would come into the larger cities, spot the products I had brought, and take home large quantities—enough to last them until their next shopping trip. I traveled quarterly to Alaska, and the sales exploded.

CHECKING IN

As I worked on selling throughout my territory and took regular trips to Alaska, I also monitored my progress. I kept the goals in front of me so I would remember them. I also called the VP of sales in New York every month. We would talk through what I had done and check if I was on track in the different areas.

These phone calls also kept me motivated, as I wanted to give a good report to the VP every time we spoke. They likely kept me in his mind too, and he saw that I was eager to work hard and reach a tough goal. I was new at the company, but since I had my sights on New York City, I thought winning the prize could be a stepping stone to eventually getting to live and work full-time there.

Walking Onstage

The months passed, and soon, it was time to get ready for the next sales meeting in New York City. I had spent the year moving as fast as I could, covering as much of my territory as possible and striving for the goals laid before me. Would it be enough to win? I was about to find out.

That year, as I again went to the beautifully decorated hotel and attended the different marketing presentations, I couldn't help but think of how much had happened during the last year. I had certainly learned an incredible amount, and I had found some uncharted markets that were beneficial to the company.

To get ready for the final event, I bought a spectacular dress. It was a cobalt blue, and it made me feel like a princess and sophisticated at the same time. When the big night arrived, I put it on and walked into the ballroom, thinking of how far I had come. I could barely make it through the dinner, and when they announced it was time to hand out the awards for the year, I sat up straight. I was ready.

They went through the different prizes ... and then it was time for the grand finale once again. The VP of sales took the microphone with Jenefer and announced that the Account Executive of the Year award would go to ... me!!

I walked onto the stage and was presented with a sash that was the same color as my dress. I could hardly believe it when the hosts gave me a Rolex watch and the incredible Tiffany plaque which was engraved to mark my win. I was in the clouds and didn't know if I would ever come down.

A New Day

The following morning, a breakfast was served for the attendees of the national sales meeting, just as it had been the previous year. I was still on such a high that I put the sash I had won over my outfit. Then I went to grab something to eat and say goodbye to the other managers and executives.

Not long after I entered the room, Jenefer and the VP of sales spotted me. They came over to me and pulled me aside, then asked me to step outside of the room. We walked out together, and then they explained, "That was last year, Terri. You have to take the sash off. Go upstairs and pack it. Hold on to it forever, but you have to start over today."

I quickly got the message! Fortunately, they had seen me shortly after I entered the room, and I didn't get too far into the breakfast to embarrass myself in front of the hundreds of other attendees. Their point was that while the sash was a great win, it was a sign of the previous year's performance. This breakfast was a sign of a fresh start, and it was time to work toward sales for the next year.

Whenever I think about the story of the L'Oréal sash, spanning from the first time I saw it being awarded to when it was given to me, I am reminded of the power of selling yourself. If you want to make great sales and achieve a goal, it starts with being yourself and being a good listener. Ask questions and engage with the other person. You'll learn what people are looking for, and then you can help them find a solution. That's how I learned about the remote shoppers in Alaska. Once I could help them get the products they wanted, they were ready to buy as much as possible.

As you interact with others, take some time to sit back and relax. If you're engaged and present a good case, the sale will come. And you could even get an award, bonus, or promotion for your hard work. Once you do, take some time to enjoy it and reflect on your accomplishments. Then get up and start the new day, ready to work hard and strive for excellence again.

Key Takeaways

- When you see a prize you want, talk to others, and find out how you can get it. That way, you'll have a road map to follow, and it could be easier to move toward your goal.
- Be ready to listen to clients and find out what they are struggling with. Once you've identified their challenges, you could come up with creative ways to help them reach a solution.
- Monitor your progress by checking in regularly, like once a month. You'll be able to see where you're on track and how you can improve the following month. Take some moments to savor your accomplishments. Then, get ready to get back to work and strive for the next goal in your sights.

CHAPTER SIX

TRUSTING THE HEART

After I won the award for the territory manager of the year at L'Oréal, I continued to follow my strategy to sell, sell, sell! I kept working at the territory I was covering in the Northwest. Based out of Seattle, I traveled to different areas, including regular trips to Alaska, where I worked through cold temperatures and occasional snowstorms (wearing stylish clothes and great heels the whole time—thanks Nordstrom!). The year that I had spent working so hard to get the award paid off, as I knew how to set goals, track sales, and monitor my progress from month to month.

Another benefit from winning the award was that my name became known in L'Oréal circles. The amazing Jenefer Lass kept mentoring me, which I greatly appreciated. In addition, I had made an impression on the VP of sales in New York. He had watched me step up and work hard to get the award I wanted.

Perhaps due to these two factors—a strong sales performance and getting recognized for my dedication and commitment to the brand—I was invited to another event in New York City. This time, it involved a lunch in the executive dining room of the L'Oréal headquarters building. I was in my late twenties at the time and so excited to be asked to come to the meeting. I knew there was a position opening that would involve managing a larger account, and I was hoping to get it. I felt ready to move up and take on more responsibilities.

The trip would lead to many more "new" moments, even though I didn't know exactly what they would be! If you are ever in a position where you have a chance to step up and try something different, I encourage you to try it if it seems exciting to you. Whatever you need to learn, you can figure out along the way. That's exactly what I did, and as I look back on that time, I am so glad I took the leap.

Leaving Seattle

At the executive lunch, I met with the VP of national sales for L'Oréal. He explained to me that JCPenney was moving its headquarters from New York City to Plano, Texas. Plano is near Dallas, and the change would involve transferring New York–based JCPenney employees to Texas.[5] L'Oréal was looking to have a manager living in the area to oversee the JCPenney account. My name had been served up as a candidate to consider.

During the lunch, I was offered the position to represent L'Oréal in Plano, Texas. It would be a promotion for me to national account sales manager with compensation incentives to manage and grow JCPenney with L'Oréal. It was a big compliment in many ways—I was gaining a good reputation within the company and being given an incredible opportunity.

---

5 Paul Richter, "J.C. Penney to Move Headquarters from New York to Dallas," *Los Angeles Times*, April 30, 1987, https://www.latimes.com/archives/la-xpm-1987-04-30-fi-2914-story.html.

As excited as I was to think about moving up in the company, I knew that going to Dallas would be hard for my family (and me too!). Even though they knew I had been dreaming of leaving Seattle, we had all enjoyed living close together. They would be saddened to see me go. For Dad especially, the news would be crushing. He was so proud of me for getting a promotion, but I knew he would miss me terribly too.

With so many mixed emotions, I turned to Jenefer to get her thoughts. She was thrilled for me, as she herself had suggested I be put in the Texas position. She said, "If you're on your way to New York City, you have to take this promotion." She could see that it would help build my experience and level up my career. Still, I could hardly bear the thought of packing up and leaving my family and friends to go to Texas.

I knew Jenefer was right, and I also was convinced the new position would be a great fit for me. I set up a plan and started packing up boxes. I would leave my hometown of Seattle, where I had grown up, learned about doing business with Dad, carried out my first jobs, and discovered that I loved selling. I would live in Texas, without any family nearby, but I promised to call Dad weekly at a minimum and stay in touch with everyone.

When I arrived in Plano, I noticed just how small it was! The city had a population of around 120,000.[6] This was a very different lifestyle than the one I was used to living in the Seattle metropolitan area, which was home to more than 2 million people at the time.[7]

---

6 "Annual Growth Rate (1980-2009) – Plano, TX USA," Civic Plus, https://content.civicplus.com/api/assets/bedda745-0396-40d4-9c58-bfeede141de9?cache=1800.

7 "Seattle Metro Area Population 1950-2024," Macrotrends.com, https://www.macrotrends.net/global-metrics/cities/23140/seattle/population.

The housing market worked in my favor when I moved to the area. I found a great home and made an offer, and it was accepted. With a place to live, I got ready to start my new job.

Launching a Tour

Just as I had jumped into other roles and learned how to succeed, I dove into this position in Texas. It was a thrill to manage the JCPenney account, which was the number one account in the division at the time. I immediately began building amazing relationships with the JCPenney team.

During the 1980s, coinciding with my time working for the company, L'Oréal started launching fragrances with Gloria Vanderbilt. JCPenney already had a long-standing relationship with the famous actress, artist, and author. For years, their stores had been stocked with Vanderbilt merchandise, including her well-known line of jeans. Then Gloria decided to branch into other areas, including shoes, scarves, and fragrances.[8]

A new perfume line of hers was scheduled to be introduced to the market while I was living and working in Plano. I immediately knew I wanted to be a part of the launch. I had met Michael Eiger, the chief marketing officer at L'Oréal in New York City, during one of my trips there. I reached out to him with some ideas that I had. We worked together and came up with a plan to orchestrate a tour. Gloria Vanderbilt agreed to appear at events, where we would sell her new fragrance "Glorious" and also promote her latest book, *Black*

8 Katherine Lam, "How Gloria Vanderbilt became a designer jeans pioneer, fashion industry leader," Fox Business, June 17, 2019, https://www.foxbusiness.com/business-leaders/gloria-vanderbilt-designer-jeans-pioneer.

Knight, White Knight. She would offer to sign copies of the book for shoppers at these events.

I was thrilled to be a part of the launch team. I had never put together a tour for a celebrity before! And yet, here I was, setting up the places she would visit and penciling in dates on the calendar. I knew it would take time and effort, but I was also sure that I could research everything and pull it off. I was compelled to get everything right, and I jumped into planning it all. We called the tour "Glorious," which coincided with the new perfume's name.

It was an immense undertaking to make arrangements for such a fashion and social icon. I knew it would be important to get all the details right. I wanted Gloria Vanderbilt to be happy right from the moment she checked into her hotel to start the tour. I began by finding out where she liked to stay and what she enjoyed having while on the road. Then I booked her accommodations and lined up special touches that I knew she would appreciate.

I got bottled water in her preferred brand to set up in the room and the flowers I knew she liked. I left a printed itinerary of the tour in her room and made sure it was on special, pretty paper so it would look nice when she arrived in Seattle.

Overall, I managed every step of that tour. And it went fabulously. Mrs. Vanderbilt arrived at her suite and was so lovely to meet. She knew how to make you feel like you were the only person she had ever known in her life. It was a true gift, and we got along beautifully. At the different stops on the tour, Gloria would offer to sign a copy of her book for customers. So many people wanted to come see her, and we sold an incredible number of perfume bottles too.

When Mrs. Vanderbilt was in Seattle, my parents and grandmother, Georgia, came to meet her. They found her just as elegant and beautiful as I did. In fact, my parents even came to another tour event to see her again. Dad was so proud of me, and he told me I had done a great job of managing everything.

Perhaps due to the success of the tour, I was given the opportunity to take on more accounts for L'Oréal. I oversaw the L'Oréal cosmetics and fragrances in other large national department stores. Every account that I took on grew! I controlled many of the key accounts for L'Oréal cosmetics, fragrance, and skin care.

> I credited these successes to my ability to establish great relationships and keep in touch with people.

I remembered dates that were special to them, like their birthdays, as Jenefer taught me, and I socialized with them every chance I had. I loved to entertain, and I would often invite people to have dinner with me during my travels to connect on a personal level.

I also used my creativity to drive sales. I was always thinking of events that we could do and fun activities we could offer to people. Certainly, the Gloria Vanderbilt tour was a wild success. So were the other events I set up. Soon I was running at least 50 percent of the national accounts for the cosmetic, fragrance, and skin care division at L'Oréal. I was only twenty-nine years old at the time.

New Opportunities

My track record at L'Oréal was becoming a line of successes. I had spent about five years working hard in Plano, and I was ready to move up again. I saw others in higher positions of management, and that's what I wanted too. I dreamed of becoming the VP of sales at L'Oréal.

With all the experience I had, I thought I would be ready to oversee others and have them report to me.

However, when I started looking for a promotion, I wasn't given one right away. Instead, I was offered a management position in a different division. L'Oréal had about fifteen divisions at the time, and I was told about an opening for me that would involve managing one of the hair divisions. When I looked into it, I realized that the accounts associated with hair were much smaller. I had been used to dealing with millions of dollars of business, and the accounts I would be managing in the hair division were just beginning. I wasn't motivated to try it, as it was hard to see it as a step up for me.

Fortunately, others had taken note of my drive and creativity. One in particular, Michael Eiger, reached out to me. He had been the chief marketing officer at L'Oréal and watched me grow the large accounts. He had left L'Oréal about six months before but had remained fond of me and had kept in touch. He and his business partner, Mark, had recently started a fragrance company. Michael said he wanted to speak to me about an opportunity at his new business. It would involve a management role, which he knew I was interested in. Specifically, he and Mark were looking for a national sales manager for their new fragrance group.

It would be a chance for me to move up, just as I was hoping to do. In the past, I had overseen accounts and had merchandisers who reported to me, setting up products and creating displays. This would be the first time I had full-time salespeople reporting to me. Michael flew me to New York to talk about it.

I was so happy to have the opportunity. I decided to accept the position and make the leap. It would mean leaving the big company of L'Oréal, complete with all the benefits and profit-sharing arrangements employees had. I would be moving to a small company with very few resources.

Little did I know that I was about to find myself in a whole new world. I soon learned that access to funds at the start-up would be very different than how it had worked at L'Oréal. I managed salespeople who were paid by commission. Suddenly, I had to figure out how to work with others who were going out and asking for the sale, rather than having accounts that depended entirely on what I did.

In many ways, it was hard to cut my teeth in these new areas of responsibility. At the same time, there were some key benefits. The company was located in New York, and they offered to move me there! I could hardly believe I would have the chance to live in the big city. I had been thinking of working my way there through L'Oréal, but this proved to be a faster route. We made an agreement that I would start traveling to New York and officially relocate there later. This would give me time to finish up at L'Oréal, arrange everything for the move, and adjust to the new company in New York. I was ready.

Start-Up Life

From my first day at the new job, I focused on what I knew best: relationships. I maintained the ones I had and worked to build new ones. I already had great connections at many of the major department stores, based on my background at L'Oréal. In particular, I had a strong relationship with Nordstrom, which has its headquarters in Seattle. Since I'm from the area, it was a natural connection. Within a year, I got a distribution set up for Nordstrom, which was a big win for a small fragrance company.

I also got involved in other aspects of the company. Michael and his business partner, Mark, told me about a legal case The Fragrance

Group had against its past VP of sales. I followed the former executive to see what was going on and was asked to be a witness. There were lawyers involved in the case, including an attorney named Bart Eagle who had agreed to represent The Fragrance Group.

I first met Bart at the company holiday party. I can still remember I was spinning around, having fun with my sales team and coworkers after having recently joined the start-up. I connected with Michael and Mark. Michael said, "Terri, I want to introduce you to our lawyers."

I was still in my little bubble of fun, having such a great time, and I couldn't figure out why lawyers would be showing up to a holiday event. Still, I followed Michael, and he introduced me to Bart and his partner, Vito. Coming from Texas and not yet settled in New York, I thought it was a bit odd to have attorneys at a holiday party. I was polite, and then went on to enjoy the rest of the evening, trying not to think too much about legalities.

For the next four months, Bart worked with the company to prepare the case and take it to an arbitration. Since I was involved, I started meeting with him at his office once every two weeks to prepare. The more I was there, the more I realized I liked him. He was really good-looking, had a great sense of humor, and dressed impeccably. The cuff links on his collared shirts were embossed with his initials, and he always wore a nice watch.

And he was an incredible lawyer. He had started his career as an assistant district attorney in Queens. He covered all sorts of cases related to big-city crimes for eight years and was a huge success in that office. However, he also followed everything by the book. He kept all his cases confidential.

To prepare for the hearing, I would arrive at Bart's office after work and stay for an hour or two. It was usually 8:00 p.m. or later by the time we finished. Rather than send me home on my own, Bart would always order a car service for me. The driver would take me back to the hotel where I stayed when I was in New York. I still hadn't moved to the big city and was traveling back and forth between Texas and New York during those months.

Over time, I grew more attracted to Bart. I also realized he didn't make any moves toward me. I always dressed up nicely for our meetings. Since he never asked me out during our meetings, I figured he probably had a girlfriend.

About two months after we met, during a time I was in New York working, my boss Michael suggested we go out for dinner. "Let's invite Bart too," he said. "We can be together around a table and casually discuss the case. Why don't you call him and see if he can come?"

My heart leaped. I was so nervous about asking, and part of me didn't want to try, as I feared what he would say. Still, I picked up the phone and called. When I got him on the line, I said, "Michael, Mark, and I are going out to dinner after we finish wrapping up here. Would you like to join us?"

"Oh, thank you," Bart replied. "I can't. I have another case that I have to continue working on this evening."

I felt so rejected. My heart sank. I was embarrassed but quickly recovered on the phone. "Oh, no problem," I said. "It was all very impromptu anyway."

I scurried back to my bosses and shared that he was working on another case. He wouldn't be joining us that evening. Inside, I thought, "He definitely has a girlfriend. Otherwise, he would just work on that other case in the morning."

The meetings continued for about two more months, and I kept going to his office every two weeks. However, by this point, I was convinced he wasn't available. I closed the door to the idea that we could be together in any way.

After preparing for the case, I was called to testify in the hearing. The date was set for a Friday right before Memorial Day weekend that year.

I got on the stand when it was my turn, and the other attorney started firing questions at me. Bart was there with Vito as well, representing the company as planned. I was told by the opposing attorney to answer certain questions with a yes or a no. I replied, "Well, actually, it's not that simple. I'll tell you what it really is like."

I went on to lay out the facts and everything I knew about the former executive of the company. I explained how I had followed him and what I had found. I testified exactly as we had prepared, and it went wonderfully. I could tell Bart and Vito were impressed with my answers.

The case was adjourned by the end of the day, and we all headed out for Memorial Day weekend. I was going to Florida to see some friends. Before I left, I wanted to check in with the salespeople at the company. The month was drawing to a close, and I needed to see if they had made enough sales for the month. I went to a phone booth and started dialing numbers.

I was on the phone for at least an hour. When I finished my last call, I hung up and started to leave. I had only gone down the hall a little bit when I saw Bart walking toward me. He had waited the entire time I was on the phone.

"Bart, wow; you're still here," I said.

"Yeah, I was just waiting for you," he replied. "I guess you had a few calls to make."

"Oh, well, it's really nice to see you again," I said.

"The next time you're in New York, do you think we could have dinner together?" Bart asked.

"I would love to!" I exclaimed. I couldn't believe he had finally asked me!

I wasn't going to let this opportunity slip by. I flew out to spend Memorial Day weekend in Florida and then returned to Texas. I was back in New York on the fourth of June. That day, Bart took me out on our first date. Soon our relationship was moving forward, as was my relocation to New York.

While I had thought that I would move to New York through my L'Oréal connections, it didn't work out that way. Still, I knew in my heart that it was the right choice to go to Plano first. It was also for the best that I left L'Oréal and joined a start-up. I learned so much about business while I was working at The Fragrance Group—and the fun times in New York were only beginning.

If you're debating whether to relocate to a new city for a different job, it's worth considering the benefits associated with your options. Maybe you have a great opportunity to move up in your career, as I did. Or perhaps you find that you want to remain close to family members who need help and wait until a new position in the area opens up.

When making a decision, listen to your heart. It will help you determine what's best for you and your loved ones.

Key Takeaways

- Set goals and track your progress if you're looking to move up in your career. When you do, others will pay attention to your dedication and achievements.
- When you gain recognition in your field, use it to open new doors. My increased visibility within L'Oréal led to a new offer and promotion.
- Embracing new roles and locations, even when they come with challenges, can significantly boost your career. Moving from Seattle to Plano, Texas, and then taking on new responsibilities at a start-up taught me how to be adaptable and figure things out.
- Taking on new challenges, like managing a tour or event, can expand your skill set and reputation. Don't hesitate to dive into unfamiliar projects–you might find that they lead to unexpected and rewarding career advancements.

PART THREE

RISK

CHAPTER SEVEN

PAYING DUES

I learned so much during my time in Texas with L'Oréal and managing the Gloria Vanderbilt tour. When I was offered a position at the fragrance start-up with the chance to move to New York City, it was really a dream come true! It marked a milestone in my career and brought new opportunities at both a personal and professional level.

Bart and I had started dating in the summer, while I was traveling from Texas to New York City to carry out my responsibilities. In October of that year, I officially relocated. I was looking forward to continuing our relationship and being closer, distance-wise, to each other.

There was a small part of me that mourned what now felt like a permanent departure from Seattle. When I had first moved to the Dallas area, it had been hard to leave my close friends and family members. No one knew for sure if I would make it to my goal of New York City or if an offer to move back home would come my way. Now, as I stepped away from life in Plano, Texas, and into the world of the nation's largest city, I knew with certainty that I would stay there. I would never return to call Seattle home. It was sad to close that chapter, but I was also ready to open a new one.

Fitting In

My whole dream of living in New York City included a vision of where my apartment would be located and how it would look. I wanted a two-bedroom place so that I could have family and friends visit. I also dreamed of a great view of the city. The building had to look nice, have a doorman, and have great amenities too. I wanted to be a part of all that New York had to offer!

However, it wasn't easy to find a place to rent. I got in touch with a real estate broker who could show me options. Unfortunately, all the apartments he presented to me were out of my price range.

During my housing search, I took a break to get away with Bart and his friends. We decided to go to the beach for the day. While we were gathered there, sitting comfortably on beach chairs, Bart asked me to share an update with them about my apartment search. I told them what I wanted, including the extra bedroom for guests.

"Two bedrooms?!" came the reply from the group.

"Yes," I went on. "I'm just having a really hard time, because it's rather expensive."

"Terri," they told me, "for what you're looking for, and for what it will cost, you might as well put your family up in the Waldorf hotel every time they visit!" The group went on to explain that for my first apartment, given the high cost of living in the city compared to other areas of the country, I would be best off looking for a place that could accommodate me.

After that conversation, I called back the broker who had been helping me find an apartment. "I'll just need a one-bedroom place," I said.

By setting different criteria, I was able to find a beautiful space for my first home in the big city. It was located in the Upper West Side on the twenty-first floor of an apartment building. It had a view of the river and downtown. It had great amenities too, including a media room and a playroom for kids.

I wanted to move some of the furnishings from my home in Plano, Texas, to the new apartment in New York. I was given a paper diagram of the place, which marked the length and width of each room. I measured everything and was sure my Texas furniture would fit. With that in mind, I signed the lease for the apartment.

My house was packed up in Plano; I headed to New York to wait for the furnishings to arrive. I was so thrilled to finally be living out my dream! Shortly after I got to my new place, my friend and boss, Michael Eiger, sent me a huge, gorgeous welcome-basket. It was filled with small items related to New York. I looked through the basket and found a pair of orange shorts and a pink, orange, and white T-shirt that read, "I love NYC." I thought it was so cute—I put it on right away!

THE WRONG MEASUREMENTS

Bart came over later that day to welcome me to New York in person. I started getting settled in my new apartment and waited for my furniture to arrive. One afternoon in October, it all came. And … hardly any of it fit.

In Plano, Texas, I had a large table in my dining room, which fit eight people. It was made of beautiful white oak wood. I loved to entertain and cook for others. I also purchased a king-size bed with large wooden posts in Texas. Placing it in the bedroom of my New

York City apartment, I quickly saw that it would take up nearly the whole space. I could step into the room and then jump into bed. There was no space on the floor to walk because the room was so tiny.

For the living room furniture, beautiful pink leather sofas arrived from Texas too. I was able to fit these, along with a glass-top table, in the New York apartment. I added a couple of stools near the kitchen counter for eating, and that was about all that fit!

What would I do with the rest of the furniture? There was no room for the dining room table with its eight chairs or the other large pieces I had moved from Texas. As I was contemplating what to do next, Bart called me. I explained to him what had happened, and he offered to come to help sort out the situation.

He found the dining room set in the hallway and me surrounded by boxes in a space that looked very cramped. I knew that according to the building policy, we weren't allowed to leave any large items in the hallways of the apartment building. We decided to talk to the management and explain what had happened and that I had missed the measurements. Fortunately, I was granted permission to leave the furniture in the hallway until I could get it picked up.

Next, I remembered that a coworker, the VP of finance, had just built a new house in New Jersey. I knew he would have more space available and that he might appreciate the furniture. I called him up and asked if he wanted it. He agreed to make arrangements to have the set picked up the following morning.

The Time of My Life

Fortunately for me, Bart loved New York City more than anyone else I knew. Through his eyes, I got to see some of the best places in the metro area. We had an amazing time on the weekends, and we took in the sights every chance we could.

At one point, Bart told me, "Terri, they always say that you'll never be alone in New York City because there are so many people." There was no truer statement. I would go out and meet people everywhere I went. I loved that it was easy to walk around and learn so much at every turn.

Bart and I became engaged after a two-year whirlwind romance filled with NYC fun and biking and travel.

THE PERFECT DRESS

Since my career was so focused on the fashion and beauty industry, I knew I wanted to get the perfect dress for the wedding. Not long after we were engaged, Bart and I had brunch together in SoHo. After we ate, I walked past the shops to look at dress options. I saw a fabulous gown hanging in the window of a boutique that sold dresses, listed as One-of-a-Kind Bride. I came to a standstill and knew immediately that it could be mine.

I asked Bart to take a walk, and I went into the shop. I asked about the dress in the window. The salesclerk told me it had just come back from a cover shoot for *Brides* magazine. It had amazing design and intricate details. I tried it on and loved it! "I'll take this one," I told the clerk.

"Do you want to try on another dress to compare?" she asked.

"No," I said, "I really want this one." It fit like a glove and was so beautiful.

The sales rep insisted I try on more, and we went through about six more dresses. After I tried them all on, I went back to the first one I had seen. It was dreamy and absolutely perfect.

We got married on November 14, 1993, in Long Island City at Water's Edge. It was a glorious night, and the Manhattan skyline was the perfect backdrop. My whole family came for it, and we had about 140 people in all. Bart and I put it on ourselves. We enjoyed preparing all the wedding details together like the flowers, band, special songs, and menu. It was our dream wedding event, and in many ways, it was a defining moment for us. We were proud that we had both found a special love together and great careers and could invite so many of our loved ones to join us for the special day.

Without Bart in my life, I don't think I would have scheduled so many fun activities. I likely would have been more focused on work. Thanks to his help, I've created strategies to live a well-balanced life (and we'll talk about this more in a later chapter).

Moving to New York City was definitely the fulfillment of a long-held dream. Still, when I got there, I faced new challenges, including finding a place, getting settled, and building a new life. I don't regret the move; even though I've changed jobs since moving there, I've never left New York City. It has become home and a place that Bart and I can enjoy together.

When you have a chance to live out a dream you've had for a long time, keep in mind that there could be some bumps you'll have to get through.

I encourage you to look for ways to overcome the challenges and ask others for help along the way. Once you've found solutions, you'll be able to appreciate the long way you've come to get to where you are.

Key Takeaways

- When you're offered a new career opportunity, especially one that aligns with your dreams, embrace it fully. Relocating for a new job can open doors both professionally and personally.
- Don't hesitate to reach out for advice or help when facing new challenges. Friends and family can provide the resources and advice you need.
- Sometimes, achieving a dream involves a certain level of compromise. Focus on the advantages and keep a positive attitude while working to find solutions.
- Take time to settle into your new life, and gradually make it your own. Enjoy exploring your new city and the opportunities it offers.

CHAPTER EIGHT

COURAGE TO FLY

I loved the chance to move into management with the start-up The Fragrance Group in New York. After a couple of years, though, I saw signs that made me think about getting another job. New companies come with unique challenges, and I could see the sales figures every month. I wasn't sure if it would survive (even though Dad's restaurant took off! Yet even he was aware of the risks involved with entrepreneurial lifestyles). So, I accepted a VP of sales role with Revlon, The Halston Group. Then I received an invite from Montblanc to interview for a job; I was compelled to go.

To avoid interrupting my work, I flew out on a weekend for the interview. I needed to travel to Hamburg, Germany, to meet with the company executives. On the flight over, I tried using a Montblanc fountain pen to see what they were like. That was when I learned not to do that in the air! By the time the plane landed, I had splattered ink all over. I had to clean up quickly and finalize my preparations for the interview.

I soon found myself speaking to a group of Montblanc management executives about the role. I was the first female they had hired for the VP of sales role. They knew of my track record for sales and my ability to drive innovation and be creative while continually building relationships. They hired me (and I knew I would figure out how to use fountain pens!)

One of the reasons they were so interested in bringing me on board was related to branding. When I joined Montblanc, the company was trying to better position itself in the luxury space. It wanted to have a prominent presence in top department and specialty stores, alongside other high-end, luxury brand names. I could use my sales background and marketing expertise to help reposition its merchandise.

First Floor Sales

When I dug into the numbers, I saw there was much to be done! Montblanc had its products selling in places like office stores and independent pen shops at the time. While that may have been great for offices, the global company set a journey to rebrand as a luxury writing instrument as step one. My new CEO of Montblanc, Stanislas de Quercize, was ready to get started on the work before us. He welcomed me as VP of sales and marketing and quickly took me under his wing (as I mentioned in chapter four). He was promoted within the Richemont Group and relocated from his home in Paris to New York City.

Stanislas had his eye on top spots in retail, starting in NYC. "Terri," he told me with his fabulous French accent, "we can't brand on the seventh floor. We must be on the main floor of Bloomingdale's 59th Street, NYC. We must have our Montblanc boutique on the first floor."

What?! I thought. Michael Gould was the chairman and CEO of Bloomingdale's at the time. How was I going to convince him that Montblanc needed space on the main floor of the department store? I knew that Stanislas was making an important point, and I understood his strategy. If the brand were higher up in the store, it wouldn't get the recognition he wanted for it. That said, I didn't know what I would say to sell the idea to Mr. Gould.

I decided to take the same approach I had used throughout my career. Just like at Russ Berrie, where I learned how to cover a sales territory and create a distribution network, and at L'Oréal, where I found ways to connect with underserved customers in Alaska, I jumped into the challenge at hand. I wrote beautiful letters with Montblanc writing instruments and on lovely stationery that were addressed to Mr. Michael Gould. I called his secretary a few times and asked for an appointment. It was truly not an easy task to set up an appointment with Mr. Gould, but I kept reaching out.

Finally, I was able to set up a time to meet with Mr. Gould. When I arrived at his office, I had my speech already prepared. I gave my pitch for having Montblanc merchandise on the main floor, and I thought it landed well. Mr. Gould even agreed to giving Montblanc a great space. The location was prime—front door, main floor left when you walked in! There was just one caveat.

"You'll have to do $1 million of business in year one," he said. If we didn't make it, he wanted Montblanc to write a check for the remaining amount.

I was happy to be given the chance to set up on the main floor, but I knew it would take something extra to get to $1 million. At the time, the company was projecting sales that were a fraction of that amount through Bloomingdale's. How could I turn a fraction of sales on the seventh floor into $1 million a year? And yet, I didn't want to have to go back to Stanislas and ask for a check at the end of the year!

Soaring Sales

I dove in and started selling! I came to Bloomingdale's nearly every Saturday for the entire year that followed. I set up a writing station and carried out fountain pen writing sessions. Weekend shoppers who walked past would often want to stop and look and try out the writing instruments. They were quite beautiful, and many people enjoyed getting a hands-on experience. The sales rolled in!

During that period, I also learned the value of exclusivity. Montblanc would create a special line of merchandise in limited editions and limited quantity. When I showed the items to customers, they were often attracted to having a chance to buy a product that wouldn't always be available and that few could access.

I went on to get Montblanc in prominent spaces in other retailers too. I contacted people I knew, held events to teach customers how to use the writing instruments, and explained the limited availability. With those tactics, the brand was shifting into luxury space—just as the company wanted.

Importantly, being with Montblanc gave me a chance to be involved in executive management. As I mentioned earlier, I learned during those years how to manage people. It takes a skill set to work with others and bring out the best in them. If you only know one strategy to motivate people, it might not work on everyone. Team members are inspired to act based on what they connect with, and that can vary from person to person. Once I knew how to listen to people and find out what they longed for, I could help them find ways to achieve it. This proved to increase productivity at the company, drive sales, and create a positive working environment.

I was proud of the role I played in helping Montblanc establish itself as a luxury brand. The company had come to be so due to my track record of increasing sales and thinking strategically to move up. It was a thrill for me to walk through department stores and see the brand featured among the other top-end ones—right where it belonged.

Moving On

I loved working with Stanislas de Quercize, the CEO at Montblanc, and will be forever grateful for the opportunities he gave me. I learned so much and saw myself grow into executive management. It was a great ride!

However, I also watched our time working together come to an end. Stanislas accepted a position that was a great opportunity for him to move up in leadership. It also meant that he moved back to Europe and wouldn't be interacting directly with me anymore on a daily basis (however, he is forever in my life).

The news was saddening; in some ways, I didn't want the climb to end. At the same time, I knew change was part of life and work. After all, I had accepted positions that led to moving far away from family and friends. I knew that moving up also meant you had to let go of the present. And as I thought about it more and new management came in, I realized … I was ready to leave too.

One of the driving forces behind this decision came from the different dynamics that entered the workplace after Stanislas left. I had grown very used to his support and encouragement. Without him, I didn't have the same voice at the table. I knew I had skills that could be used in a higher leadership role, I just had to find a path that would allow me the chance to apply them.

Signing the Contract

Up to this point in my career, I had worked my way up the corporate ladder. From Russ Berrie to L'Oréal and Montblanc, I was very familiar with large infrastructures and an extensive chain of command. Through coaching and experience, I was able to navigate executive management. I had always been able to hustle, to set sales goals and go after them. I knew how to figure out new opportunities too. I would jump in, carry out the research needed to understand a responsibility or task, and then get the job done.

Others in the industry had noticed this. Perhaps this is why Mark and Candy Udell of London Jewelers recommended me for the job. Mark and Candy were running the most successful jewelry retail business in the US at the time. They are both incredible in their industry, consistently making smart decisions as a retailer. I had worked with them while I was at Montblanc, and they had seen my work ethic. When Mark and Candy learned that a family-run jewelry company was looking for help, they shared my name.[9]

This position would be my first time joining a family business. It was owned by two of the most talented jewelry designers to this day. I would be working alongside its founders, Sybil and David Yurman. They started their namesake company in 1980. David's designs first focused on innovative collections of the renowned silver cable bracelets, combined with earrings, rings, and necklaces. He used

9 Ashley Davis, "Retailer Hall of Fame 2023: Candy Udell," *National Jeweler*, October 19, 2023, https://nationaljeweler.com/articles/12380-retailer-hall-of-fame-2023-candy-udell.

semiprecious stones to create pieces with new combinations in shape, texture, and color.

During the years that followed, their brand grew. Sybil was a brilliant marketer, and David was a phenomenal designer. They were at a place in their business that required more help, and they were smart enough to know that and acknowledge it. The company was ready to go to the next level. They just needed somebody to take it there and partner with them.

They asked me to bring in my expertise and help grow the business. Before signing me on, however, they had me go through a rigorous vetting process. Part of this included going out for lunch with Sybil. While we ate together (and she evaluated me!), she confessed to me, "I've never hired someone for such a high-ranking position before. Does this feel like we are getting married?"

I responded, "Maybe, Mrs. Yurman, but don't worry; it will be good."

I knew I would be a great fit for the role, and I brought up points during our discussion to help Sybil see that too. I was known as a relationship builder, and I had just spent years revitalizing the Montblanc brand. Others had seen that I really cared about the people involved, and that these strong connections made me a powerful force in the industry. Most of all, I knew how to orchestrate sales and manage the business side too.

Fortunately, Sybil and David also saw this. They hired me, and I walked into a new chapter of my life. For eight years, it would be a ride that was more incredible than I ever imagined. I smile as I reflect on all we accomplished together.

As I look back at this time of my life, I realize the great strides I took in managing people and learning how to operate at the executive level. I drew on my years of experience in other roles, along with the new teachings I was gathering, to carry out my new responsibilities. If you find yourself suddenly in a higher position, I encourage you to find coaching and resources to help you build your skill set. Once you do, you'll be ready to lead with heart—and others will appreciate that too.

Key Takeaways

- When you come across signs that it's time to move on, don't hesitate to explore new opportunities. Taking on something different could help you develop even more as a leader.
- When you're selling, it's not just about getting the right numbers so you can say you reached your goal. It's about building relationships, working hard to reach goals, and being open to new ideas.
- Try to cultivate strong relationships, continue to reach out, and keep a smile on your face. Michael Gould at Bloomingdale's saw that I was pleasant to work with and that I was ready to give my best effort.
- When you find yourself in a higher position, look for coaching and resources to develop your skills and lead from the heart.

CHAPTER NINE

SURRENDERING TO THE DREAM

I couldn't wait for my first day of work in the office of David Yurman jewelry in New York. At the time, the company was renting a space at 501 Madison Avenue. The office covered about ten thousand square feet. There were around thirty employees working on the three floors set aside for the office.

When the day arrived, I walked into the space and found a very busy business, with phones ringing in customer service and salespeople juggling. The reason for this stemmed from the fact that jewelry retailers throughout the country wanted what David Yurman was selling—and they wanted it right away.

However, the orders were piling on so fast that the company couldn't keep up with them. David had recently introduced the cable bracelet, and it was an immediate hit and success. During that first day, Sybil took me around the office. She introduced me to the team members and showed me the different departments they had. I was excited to meet everyone and to understand how the company was operating.

While making this initial tour, I entered an area that had papers all over the floor. Upon closer inspection, I realized the sheets were coming off the paper tray of a fax machine. The machine sat on a desk and received messages. However, the papers were going through the machine so quickly that they were spilling onto the floor.

I pointed to the papers I saw strewn around us. "Mrs. Yurman, what are these?" I asked.

"Oh, those are the orders."

Retailers from around the country were sending in orders for David Yurman jewelry. They wanted to have the hottest items around! There was just one problem: the orders were coming in so fast, piling on the floor, that the company couldn't keep up. I thought, "That's money lying on the floor!"

I knew we would have to do something about this issue, and soon. After all, the buyers didn't want their orders to get lost. If they sent a fax and never heard back, they would be upset.

In fact, I realized this was already happening when I went into the customer service area. There were about five people on the phones in this department. They were dealing with retailers who were calling in and asking what had happened to their order. While I knew we would have to change the system, I also recognized the potential. Everyone wanted David Yurman jewelry!

We weren't running around, trying to make a sale. The sales were coming in, and they were coming in fast! I thought, "This could be the start of an incredible success story."

Once I had finished the initial tour of the office, I thought about the next steps. I knew the top priority of the moment was to better manage the orders coming in. With so many requests lying on the floor, some were bound to get lost or thrown out. We had to have a better way to accept and process orders.

I went to Mrs. Yurman and the VP of finance with my first request. "Could we get two more fax machines?" I asked.

I got approval, and soon, we had a total of three fax machines to take orders. I then lined up the rest of the process, which included having someone review each request that came in. They would input the details of the order into the computer system. It would then be channeled over to the production team. It may have been a simple setup, but it was a significant improvement from the single, overloaded fax machine.

I was used to being at corporations that used much more sophisticated systems for ordering. And yet, I just loved the challenge of finding a way to get business done. Getting those new fax machines and helping to line up a process was only one of the many new experiences I was about to have. The company was ready to soar high, and I was too.

A Huge Success

My time at David Yurman was full of challenging and yet very positive growing pains as the business became a huge hit in the industry. I needed to find ways to manage the high demand for their signature cable bracelets. David had landed on a design that appealed to so many women: moms could wear the bracelet to pick up their kids from school, office workers could put it on for their day job, and anyone going out for the evening could dress up their outfit with the jewelry.

While it wasn't easy, it was a great feeling to be part of a success story as it was taking place. The David Yurman team seemed to be just as excited as I was. Everyone got along well. In a way, we were really all part of the Yurman family, and we grew together. We brought on more team members to help the company keep up with orders. In the meantime, David started designing additional collections, and each one did very well.

As I mentioned, Sybil was a brilliant and natural marketer; she had great instincts. She understood our advertising images should reflect a lifestyle of relaxed American luxury. She knew the models in our campaigns should feel beautiful yet natural, and that the photos would need to move you. She partnered with creative director David Lipman who understood that she was in fact David Yurman's muse, and the models should wear their jewelry the way Sybil would in her everyday life. Together Sybil and David Lipman would go on to hire famed photographer Peter Lindbergh. They would cast models that expressed the energy of relaxed luxury with a sense of joy. Our campaigns for over a decade went on to feature bold-name supermodels like Amber Valletta, Kate Moss, and Naomi Campbell, and newer, undiscovered models that were of the editorial moment. Soon advertising images of Amber and Kate styled in David Yurman jewelry filled the pages of top publications. Readers loved it! They hurried into the boutiques with the magazines in hand in search of the latest Yurman style.

This move only created higher demand for the company. I could handle the growing pains as I'm very resourceful and worked hard to figure out how to do new things. We were continually dealing with challenges such as people not having enough resources, not having enough capacity to fill orders, and not having enough staff or space. Every day there was a new issue to deal with, and I loved finding the solutions.

Given this, Sybil and David leaned on me to manage the escalating business, and this included finding new office space when we outgrew the 501 Madison location. I had never moved a company before! But I went out and started looking at properties with the Yurmans.

We soon found a huge, beautiful space on Vestry Street. It covered about sixty thousand square feet, and I immediately knew it would be a great fit. It was a raw space, and I led the way to making it into the David Yurman headquarters. David and Sybil brought in the creative part, setting the tone for how it would look. I contributed by overseeing the logistical parts of the project, which included negotiating the lease, working with lawyers to cover all the legal matters, hiring the moving company, and carrying out the move.

We continued to leap forward, growing and becoming an even stronger company. With branding in place and our advertising creative rivaling the most impactful in any magazine, it was time to fine-tune our communication strategy. Knowing this was an essential part of success we hired HL Group, a boutique public relations firm, founded by Hamilton South and Lynn Tesoro. They were dialed into the editors and taste makers of the moment and would collaborate on how to craft our unique message in the market. We were a brand that sat squarely in the space that crossed over from fine jewelry to fashion. David Lipman and HL Group were instrumental in transforming the company and securing our spot as a leading American luxury brand.

I also built new relationships with some of the top media publishers and editors of the day, which included creating a friendship with Lou Cona, the President of the Condé Nast Media Group, which includes well known media brands such as Vanity Fair and Vogue. I reached out to him to discuss buying a schedule of ads, featuring David Yurman products to be included in the most prestigious front pages and back covers of the influential Condé Nast media brands, right alongside the major cosmetic brands and famous watches. He appreciated my friendly, direct style and helped line up the promotions I was asking for.

Over time, he asked me to events, where I continued to network with others. Lou invited me to the Oscars, including the evening and after-hours parties. I also made friends with Amy Churgin, the publisher of Architectural Digest. Through that relationship, I set up more advertisements for David Yurman that could reach the brands audience. Tom Florio of Vogue/Condé Nast and Giulio Capua were gems to have as marketing partners, as was Steve DeLuca.

As business increased, so did the team size. I worked with key instrumental executive leadership and grew a team I was proud to have with me. I hired Carol Pennelli as senior VP of sales and Maria Valim as national sales manager, Carl Barbato was VP of retail, and Deborah Klemm came on as VP of finance, and she continued to join me in two additional roles over the years. Claire Gilvar was my executive assistant and went on to join me in future marketing management over the years. Janet Hayward, Tracy Squillante, Danielle Twersky, Scott Vogel, Victor Bocarossa, Evert DeGraeve, Susie Kimball, Dawn Pearson, Cathy Fatta-Marsh, Kate Harrison, and Gladys Byrnes were also longtime David Yurman management team members, just to name a few! I loved the team, and we were magical together.

When I started working at David Yurman, the company didn't have a retail store. They sold collections to independent jewelry stores and department specialty stores. With me on board, I oversaw the opening of their first retail store. I had already been involved in opening a place, as I had established spaces for Montblanc during my time there.

For David Yurman, I found the perfect location on Sixty-Fourth and Madison Avenue. It was about 1,500 square feet, and I arranged to have it open the day after Thanksgiving, the biggest shopping day of the year. It was—beyond our wildest dreams—a huge success.

I went on to open twelve more stores during my time with David Yurman. All of them did very well, with shoppers flocking to the retail locations to purchase jewelry. I managed the retail operations along with the wholesale segment, which consisted of independent jewelers. To do all of this, I relied on my longtime and valuable friendships. I worked with top executives at places like Neiman Marcus, Bloomingdale's, and Saks Fifth Avenue along with important jewelers, including London Jewelers, Finks Jewelers, Reis-Nichols, and Diamond Cellar, to name just a few.

The Best Career

In so many ways, I was living my dream job. It was awesome, and I loved it. I had so much fun, and I thrived on the accomplishments that I was able to make every day. The highs were so incredible that it was almost addicting to work there (in a good way!). It was a bit like living in the land of the beautiful; I was surrounded by amazing jewelry, people who were fun and smart, and amazing opportunities to grow.

It was a "boots on the ground business," and I was passionate about building relationships in person with our customers, the media world, and the industry at large. Several times a year I attended premier trade shows, including the Jewelers Circular Keystone (JCK) show in Las Vegas and Baselworld, the largest global jewelry and watch fair in Basel, Switzerland. We would display David's latest collections and draw crowds of onlookers. I adored traveling to Basel and my accommodations, a gorgeous apartment with a view of the flowing Rhine River.

Travelling to trade shows was incredible, and the business we wrote—even better!

As I look back at that time, I can recall doing so many tasks that I had never carried out before. When David and Sybil would ask if an idea of theirs was possible, I would simply volunteer to help. "No problem; I'll take care of it," I would say.

Even if I didn't have the knowledge to immediately solve the problem, I knew how to ask others. I would use my network or make phone calls until I could see a path forward. While I started as the executive vice president, I moved up to take on the role of the COO of the company. With David as the CEO and Sybil as president, the three of us were an awesome team.

One of the keys to the success of David Yurman was the ability to appeal to a wide market. After the original cable bracelet, David kept designing like mad, and everything he made that hit the market was huge. Silver ice, pink ice, blue ice, fine jewelry, watches, and a men's line all followed the cable bracelet. Everyone wanted to wear what he designed. He had cracked a code and found a way for everyone to see, "She can wear it." The company had grown by extreme leaps and bounds in sales and profits.

David, for his part, was always changing, always evolving, and consistently a modern designer. The team members and I got to enjoy his new designs when they came out. As a team, we were given "friends and family samples" sales, and the pieces were beautiful. The Yurmans also gifted me some amazing pieces.

Moreover, they taught me and others how to style it with clothing. This was new in the industry at the time. When I opened retail stores, I hired people that had a background in fashion. I didn't need jewelry professionals; I wanted someone who could show shoppers how to wear the pieces. We taught customers how to layer items, such as putting different necklaces together and adding on a bracelet to go with the ensemble.

To this day, I love to walk past the boutiques and see David Yurman jewelry. It's as gorgeous as ever. Still, as I had seen with Stanislas, nothing lasts forever, no matter how great it seems at the time. I had learned during my time at David Yurman that I could solve complex issues and lead during periods of high growth. I felt strong and ready to take on a new leadership role. What that would be, I was about to find out. We'll open that portion of my life, and the learning I gained through it, in the next chapter.

Key Takeaways

- Look for inefficiencies that can be corrected and prioritize what must be done to help a business meet its goals when you take on a new role. You can then start leading others through changes to streamline processes.
- Pay attention to the different strengths that each team member brings. At David Yurman, David specialized in design while Sybil had her eye on the marketing. I brought in operational, sales and marketing, and branding expertise and positioned the company so it could grow.
- During chaotic times, look for what you can do each day. Treat others like family members so that everyone can contribute together and have fun at the same time.
- Don't be afraid to try different strategies to see what works. Even if it hasn't been done before in your industry, it could be exactly what your company needs to differentiate itself from the competition.

PART FOUR

LEARN

CHAPTER TEN

BECOMING THE CEO

The phenomenal growth that the David Yurman brand went through during my years with the company did not go unnoticed. Its jewelry became recognized as an American success story, and customers paid attention to the continuous new designs it produced. It gained the top spot in the branded luxury market. And I helped it get there.

After eight years with David Yurman, serving as the COO for much of that time, another opportunity arose. It was also in the jewelry industry, though it had the number two spot among competitors. The company was a business competitor to David Yurman and specialized in handcrafted artisan jewelry. I was offered the position of president and CEO. I would have the chance to take on even more leadership by reporting to the board and guiding a growth strategy for the brand on my own.

The Story

One of the attractions of the business, for me, was its powerful background. It was founded in 1975, and from the beginning, all of the jewelry has been made by hand. The business invested during the 1970s and 1980s in learning from local artisans in Bali. From them, the business mastered jewelry-making techniques that had been used on the island for centuries. It also developed an approach to creating sustainable pieces.[10]

Rather than mining silver and gold to use for the creation of jewelry, artisans at the business use 100 percent reclaimed silver and gold. The metals are melted down and given new life, and any excess scraps that are generated during the production of jewelry are recycled and reused in future pieces. Its entire process is so focused on reducing waste that less than 1 percent of its materials end up in a landfill.[11]

In Bali, the artisan workshop is built out of low-impact, native materials, including bamboo and adobe. It is situated on a four-hundred-acre organic permaculture farm with rice paddies throughout it. All wastewater from the workshop is recycled and used to water the farm. Its Kapal Bamboo Boutique is made of bamboo and native grasses. It is designed to "float" over the Subak, which is an irrigation system that waters the rice fields in Bali. This water infrastructure flows under the Kapal.[12]

I loved that the brand focused on giving back to the community and supported local artisans in Bali. The business promoted conservation and sustainability. When customers bought a piece of jewelry, they knew they were helping out artisans and their families. They

10 "John Hardy: The Story," John Hardy, accessed May 22, 2024, https://johnhardy.com/en-uk/pages/sustainable-luxury.

11 "John Hardy: The Story."

12 "John Hardy: The Story."

could also be sure that they were interacting with a company that cared about the environment and wanted to preserve it.

Looking back on my career, I've always been attracted to brands that have a story to tell. I can get passionate about these backgrounds and what they mean. I can then translate them to help consumers understand the message and importance. I want others to see what the brand represents and the story behind the face of the company.

That's a point I like to make to others who are looking to take on a new position. I always advise against taking on just any role. I encourage you to find something that you can be passionate about.

> Look at the story behind the brand. If you love it, you'll be motivated to share it with others. Also remember that you can always improve the story. You might be able to add better marketing, upgrade the product, or create a different design. If a brand has a great base storyline, you can work to take it to the next level.

Under my direction, the business brand grew substantially. I professionalized and organized every area of the company from the ground up. By sharing the story of the brand with others, we found ways to connect with shoppers and give them a chance to support local artisans.

If you're offered a position as CEO, be ready for anything! I found unexpected surprises in my new role, ranging from the warehouse-style office to walking on a log bridge over water buffalo in Bali! When facing each issue, I put on a good face and looked for ways to make the best of the situation. If you do the same, you'll find ways to grow the business and shine in your industry.

Like the other changes I had made in the past, I saw this as a way to move up. I appreciated the chance to have the title of CEO and an incentive plan for a future sale of the company for the first time, even though I was aware it would come with more responsibilities. For me, it was the next step for what I wanted to accomplish. I saw it as an opportunity to lead and manage a company on my own.

The board wanted to see double-digit growth, and they saw me as the person who could help provide that. I loved the challenge and was eager to chase a new goal. I accepted the position and soon found myself making big changes both in New York City and abroad.

Designing a Space

The US Sales, Marketing, and Operations departments for the business were based in New York City, but the designers of the company lived in Bali. This meant I would be carrying out much of the office work in the city. The position involved regular travel to Bali, along with trips to visit retailers throughout the US.

When I accepted the position, I hadn't yet had the chance to see the inside of the offices for the business in New York City. So, the first day of the job, I took a tour of the space to see it and get to know the people working at the company. I immediately noticed the space could use help.

In this case, it really needed Terri love. From the decor to the environment, everything in that space was ready for improvement! It wasn't organized in a very professional way. The setup was ample, and yet it didn't feel very welcoming to the employees or visitors. In fact, it looked a bit like a warehouse on the inside. I wanted to give it the love and attention it needed so that when a person walked in, they felt good.

This was an exciting project to take on. Even though I had moved an office before, during my time at David Yurman, this was my first chance to put my own touches on the space. I helped pick out new furniture that fit with the brand. I also arranged the environment so that it felt inviting and warm to the team. I put my touch on every single department of the office.

I was very proud of the changes we made. About a month after I arrived, I held a launch party at the Ritz-Carlton on Central Park South. I used the event as a chance to welcome retailers and do a kickoff. We had amazing decorations, a great menu, cocktails, and an atmosphere of hospitality and sustainability. Models wore the jewelry throughout the evening. I wanted to show everyone how it would be going forward at the business.

I didn't have much help at the beginning, but by this point in my career, I was used to being very resourceful! I hired a few people who had worked for me in the past. They joined the company, and we rallied and pulled together to make improvements.

While I loved improving the office in New York, I also knew I had to learn about the rest of the company. Shortly after joining, I made my first trip to Bali. Getting there would mean taking a twenty-five-hour flight. In Bali, I would meet with the owners and the designers. I would have a chance to see the artisans at work, and I couldn't wait.

Visiting Bali

While the flight was long, as soon as I arrived in Bali, I saw how fabulous it was. The island was amazing, and I looked forward to exploring it. With the job position, I knew I would be traveling there about three times a year and staying for about ten days each trip. For my first stay, it was important to establish relationships with the designers and owners so we could lay a foundation and build on it during the next visits.

For this initial trip, I was scheduled to stay with the owners in their home. To help me get a sense for the island, I was taken on a nature outing. We started by walking through the fields in the area. Then we rode bikes through incredible tropical scenery. For the last stretch, we went on a walk. By this point, I was having the time of my life! I was surrounded by stunning beauty at every turn.

At the end of the walk, we came to a log that we had to cross. It was set up over a river, and underneath, I could see water buffalo in the water! We had to go over the log bridge to get to the owners' house, which was where I would be staying. There was no turning back!

I looked over my outfit; I was definitely not prepared for this part of the hike! I had on cute sneakers, little shorts, and a small top. Even though I was very active and had been a cheerleader, I didn't know if I would make it across the log. I didn't want to end up in the water. The others with me assured me that the water buffalo weren't dangerous; still, I didn't want to have to be pulled out of the river if I fell in.

I gathered up my courage and started walking tentatively on the log. I put my feet side by side and moved them a little at a time to get across. Finally, I reached the other side. I made it! I could tell by the reaction of the others in the group that they admired my willingness to try and were ready to start working together.

One of the lessons I learned from that first trip to Bali was how much of a difference it made for me to be adaptable and embrace the unexpected. The island was incredibly beautiful, and it was a unique place to visit. As a leader, I was able to show I enjoyed it and could work through the different challenges that came up, like crossing a log bridge over a river filled with water buffalo. Even if everything doesn't go as planned, you can take steps to show you can get through it. Others will notice and be ready to follow your lead.

By approaching challenges with a positive and resilient mindset, you not only earn the respect of your team but also set the tone for how others handle adversity. This trip reinforced the idea that the journey to building strong relationships and a successful brand is rarely straightforward. By adapting to new environments and experiences, you can foster trust and drive growth.

A Hands-On CEO

As CEO at the business, I quickly realized the need to be both strategic and hands-on. When you're in a leadership position, you're not just guiding the overall direction of the company. You're also responsible for ensuring that every aspect of the business reflects the brand's core values. This means being deeply involved in everything. I wanted to shape the brand's story while restructuring the workspace to improve morale and productivity.

In addition, I showed others that you need to do more than just set goals from a distance; it's about being engaged with every level of the company, from the boardroom to the artisans. By connecting the brand's vision with day-to-day operations and leading by example, you can inspire your team, align everyone with the brand's mission, and drive growth. This hands-on leadership approach, combined with strategic vision, helped me build a strong brand in a short amount of time.

Key Takeaways

- Taking on the role of CEO gives you a chance to significantly impact a company's direction. Be ready to set a strategy and follow through to reach goals.
- You can improve productivity and morale by investing in a workspace that reflects the brand's story and makes employees feel valued.
- Look for the brand's story and be ready to share it with customers to create a connection. You can also find ways to improve a story by creating a better product, design, or marketing tactic.
- Take on unexpected situations with a resilient mindset. When others see you react in a calm, assured way, they'll be more likely to respect you and follow you.

CHAPTER ELEVEN

A LESSON IN RESILIENCE

During my time at David Yurman, I had ridden an incredible wave of opportunity and led the company to reach sales that amazed the jewelry industry. The competitor to David Yurman was not the only company that had spotted my incredible track record and the way the brand skyrocketed under my leadership. We became a phenomenon in the market, and our success was widely known. In fact, this is why the competitor had reached out to me in the first place—David Yurman was the top jeweler at the time, and the competitor's team was hoping to gain that title. They put me in the CEO seat, and I helped them start that climb.

A Suffering Industry

I joined the business in 2005, and under my watch, sales climbed. As the years went on, however, that would change, and other factors that were outside of my control entered the scene. Around 2008, when the Great Recession hit, the jewelry industry entered a downturn along with the rest of the global economy. Worried about what would come next, consumers stopped spending on luxury items. After a peak of nearly $30.8 billion in sales in 2007, retail jewelry store sales fell by 16.6 percent over the next two years to $25.7 billion. The average purchase per client dropped from $102.31 in 2007 to $83.77 in 2009.[13]

During my time at the business, I grew into my new position of CEO and realized I loved being at the top. Still, change is constant, and the jewelry industry was undergoing significant shifts. In 2008, the founder made a significant decision. He sold his stake in the firm to the company president and the creative director.

At the time, it was announced that I would continue as CEO of the business in the USA. The president, who was based with the company headquarters in Hong Kong, would oversee international expansion to places such as China, Japan, Russia, and the Middle East.14 The jewelry would continue to be crafted in Bali. A private equity firm backed the deal.

Not long after these changes took place, I attended a meeting with the new leadership. I came into it as the CEO of the company. When I walked out, I no longer had a job.

I was completely blindsided.

During the meeting, I tried to ask questions, and I wanted to learn. I wanted to learn the reasoning behind the decision, but I was shut down. I shared that the changes made no sense to me at all. Still, there was no budging on the other end. Any discussion would be a waste of time and energy. The decision had already been made, whether I liked it or not. I left that meeting without a position or

13 Conor Redmond, "Jeweler Tactics: What the 2008 Great Recession Can Teach Us About Covid," *Instore Mag*, May 4, 2020, https://instoremag.com/jeweler-tactics-what-the-2008-great-recession-can-teach-us-about-covid-19/.

14 Sophia Chabbott, "John Hardy Founder Sells Stake in Firm," *WWD*, July 10, 2007, https://wwd.com/feature/john-hardy-founder-sells-stake-in-firm-490613-2038067/.

title. I was overflowing with hurt, anger, and a feeling that I had been deceived. I had been completely unprepared to receive the news.

If your mouth just dropped, you are reacting in a similar way to others I have told (I couldn't believe it either!). The termination was so unexpected and so abrupt that I really did not see it coming in any way. I was completely and utterly stunned to find out I would no longer be involved with the company and that no one was willing to talk to me about it. As a salesperson, I was very accustomed to starting conversations and continuing them at a later point. Imagine my shock when I found out there would be no negotiation or opportunity to rethink the decision and keep my position at the company.

In a sense, it was perhaps a natural move that the business started looking for ways to carry out operations differently. It was clear that difficult times would be ahead with a global recession underway. The private equity that backed the changes at the company was looking at the financial aspects too. Cutting a position would save on costs and could have been seen as an important move in a down market.

The Emotional Toll

When I walked out of that meeting after having been 150 percent surprised by the news, everything seemed surreal. I had trusted the others in leadership and had completely missed any signs that changes would be made. I couldn't believe the scene that had just unfolded before my eyes and that I was now unemployed.

I managed to get myself into a taxi to go home and then I called Bart. When he answered, I said, "You're not going to believe this ..." I went on to explain what had just happened.

As I expected, he couldn't comprehend it either. There was silence on the other end of the line. As a lawyer, my husband is usually never at a loss for words. That day, however, after he heard my story, he was quiet.

Then slowly, he spoke. "Come to my office," he began. "Let's sit down and look at the paperwork." I went over to his office as he suggested. Together, we started deciphering the event that had just occurred and turned my life upside down.

By the next morning, the news was all over the jewelry industry. I always advise others to not read your own press, and I can assure you, it's very helpful during situations such as this one! It can be better to not know. If you do look, keep in mind that by the next day, there will be different headlines. Readers will be looking for the next crisis to follow, and yours can fade into the past. That's what happened in my case.

It was hard not to look at what had been written (and I did take a peek!). I also remembered that the headlines had shared big news at other points in my career. The publications had been quick to tout when I had been promoted to other positions and hired by other companies. They would soon move on to someone else.

During the next hours, the consequences of the termination started to hit me hard. Soon, some of my closest friends started to call me. Marnie McBryde, my longtime friend, rang me up. Marnie, as the owner of a leading executive search firm, had been the one to place me in the job at the competitor to David Yurman. She wanted to check on me and see how I was doing. Amy R. Churgin, another very dear friend and the publisher of *Architectural Digest*, reached out too. While they empathized with me over the tough situation, they also asked what my plans were. They wanted to help me start thinking of doing something immediately to improve the situation.

Both Marnie and Amy were right, and I needed to move on. I am so thankful for longtime friendships and for those in my life who I can count on during both the good and hard times. They, like others, had watched me rise to the top of the industry. My career had really started as a salesclerk in a drugstore, and I had moved all the way to the CEO but walked out of a meeting having lost the title.

Now, years later, I have perhaps a better perspective on the situation and have grown from the lessons I learned while going through it. I went on to continue to build my career and take on more leadership roles. Still, as I recall this moment in my life, I can't help but feel the sting again.

If you are in a leadership role, know that hard knocks will come! Even though I love to keep a positive, fun, and slightly sassy attitude, the truth is that challenges are real. It's worth spending some time unfolding the backstory to this critical moment in my career and to reflect on the steps I took to get through it. As you face low points in your career (and they will come!), you can draw comfort in knowing that it is possible to go on, to pick yourself up, and to move forward. It may be terribly painful at first, but it will get better with time. And the path you choose could even end up taking you to new heights and accomplishments!

Being Unemployed

As I worked through the intense flood of emotions during the days and weeks that followed, I learned that for leaders in high positions, falling is not only a possibility, but it can also be a tough reality. So many leaders have to face steep challenges, and they also have to move on.

In my case, in the aftermath of the termination, I knew I was entitled to receive unemployment benefits. To get the paycheck I was due, I would have to go to a nearby office. It felt so humiliating to go through these steps. I had spent my career moving my way up, had become a CEO, and now would have to pick up payments for not having a job. It was such an embarrassing thought.

While obviously I wanted to return to the workforce, it was also important for me to find the right opportunity. Rather than jumping at any job, I chose to take my time and look for something that might be a good fit. With that in mind, I headed to the unemployment office to check in. I remember riding the subway to save on transportation costs and walking into the place to receive my compensation.

Incidentally, through the unemployment office, I was selected to participate in an accountability program to find a new job. This meant that every time I went in to give an update on my job search, I had to talk about what I had done during the last weeks and how my search was going. In a way, it was a good and rigorous schedule to be on, as it held me responsible for my actions. Of course, I've always been a hard worker and a fighter. Still, I was reeling from the shock of being let go, and it wasn't easy to think about jumping back into the executive world.

There were other factors at play during that time too. The job market was pretty slim, as the Great Recession caused many companies to pull back and tighten up rather than hire and push toward growth. This was especially true for luxury brands. Customers were looking to save their money and not spend on "extras" like jewelry and cosmetics.

A few weeks into this new schedule of searching for a job and heading to the unemployment office to report on my findings, I thought, *Terri, you had better find a bright spot in this.* I had a strong network in both the business world and my personal life. I could draw on those connections and lean into the support of my friends and loved ones. I also had a track record of finding ways to be successful; surely, I could overcome this challenge too.

I will always be overwhelmed with gratitude for the close friendships during that time, for the people who called me and asked, "What are you doing?" They helped me see that there was no time to feel sorry for myself. Going through the process, I valued my close circle who were ready to stick with me and be there for me during the hard times.

Jumping In Again

To my advantage during my days of unemployment was the fact that I had already built a name for myself in multiple industries. Others had seen how resourceful I am and how I had worked in various areas of the luxury market. I knew how to build a brand, I knew how to sell, and I knew how to work hard. I just needed to find the next challenge that would give me a thrill—something to figure out and get the satisfaction of watching it grow. In other words, I was ready to start down the path to my next success.

I took some time to update my LinkedIn page. I also spent considerable effort thinking about what sort of dream job I wanted next. What would excite me? What would be thrilling to pursue? What business could I transform next?

When I was ready, I started reaching out seriously and pursuing opportunities. I let others know I was available and ready to take on a new challenge. While I had been let go, one thing was certain: the next company to take me on would not be disappointed! I wanted to continue to move up and find my next opportunity.

Key Takeaways

- Part of leadership involves being prepared for unexpected challenges, as even the most successful careers can face sudden setbacks.
- When you are hit with a sudden change, it's natural to experience a wide range of emotions. Take the time you need to sort through them and lay out a plan, so you have something to guide your next days.
- Lean into your close circle when you need it, as friends and family can provide both emotional support and practical advice to help you get back into your game.
- Take on unexpected situations with a resilient mindset. When others see you react in a calm, assured way, they'll be more likely to respect you and follow you.

CHAPTER TWELVE

REINVENTING (AGAIN)

After spending time getting myself back together after my unexpected resignation, I was ready to roll up my sleeves and dive back in. I already knew how to make a brand pop! Now I just needed the right one to come calling.

As it turned out, that's exactly what happened. When my phone rang and I saw it was my good friend, Marnie McBryde, I was excited. She has always been in my corner. Thinking she was checking up on me to see how I was doing, I answered, getting ready for a great conversation. She definitely gave me something to think about!

She said, "Terri, I have this amazing job opportunity as president and CEO, and I think you would be awesome for it. It's with F. Schumacher."

"Well, that sounds fabulous," I said. I knew nothing about Schumacher at the time, but I trusted her judgment. When I did some research, I realized the company was owned by the Schumacher family and had a prestigious history. It had branded itself as a luxury name in the home decor space for high-end designer fabric, trim, and furniture. However, over the years, its products had become associated with an older demographic, often mentioned in the same breath as "my grandmother's wallpaper." One of my key tasks would be to reenvision Schumacher and bring it to the modern world.

The possibilities appealed to me, and I knew I had found my next challenge. Thinking about my career, I could see how it had moved from cosmetics to writing instruments, into jewelry, and then to the home furnishings world. I had reinvented myself before, and I could reinvent myself—and another company—again.

I was ready to jump in. And that's exactly what I did.

Building Key Relationships

While I wasn't familiar with the home interior design industry, I've always had an eye for knowing how to make great products sell. I love to multitask and keep a pulse on the different departments. I always have a hand on the Sales team, which is especially important to me, because that's what represents the company. In addition, I love reaching out and meeting new people in the industry. It's also valuable to maintain existing relationships and engage with others who are fun and interesting.

As one of my first steps, I started to contact others in the industry and to get in touch with the popular magazine editors at the time. I read up on *Architectural Digest*, *VERANDA*, and *Elle Decor*, which were flagship publications for the home industry. I gained an understanding of the who the leading designers were. I came across some extraordinary individuals who did magnificent work—Timothy Corrigan, Martyn Lawrence Bullard, and Mary McDonald, just to name a few.

I knew we needed to modernize the Schumacher brand and that I would need assistance doing so. I started to draw on the relationships I was developing to see if I could align the company with some of the industry's most innovative and respected designers. In my efforts, I made friends with these designers and shared special times with them. For instance, Timothy Corrigan and I became very close, and I grew to admire his work greatly. Timothy is a top global designer and regularly is hired to style homes and mansions globally that are off the charts.

Timothy invited Bart and I to stay in his chateau in the Loire Valley, France. Everything was furnished in an out-of-this-world amazing design, and we were given the most magnificent bedroom I had ever seen. It looked like a place for a princess!

We spent four glorious days at his chateau, and Timothy had invited other design industry friends to join us as well. The top designers saw what I was trying to do at Schumacher, and they wanted to be a part of it. They could see the opportunity—working together would mean a lot of marketing for them too. We could have a win-win situation.

For instance (just to name a few), we developed and launched the Timothy Corrigan for Schumacher collection. We also partnered to carry out the Martyn Lawrence Bullard for Schumacher collection and the Mary McDonald for Schumacher collection. Change was definitely underway, and I was excited about what the future could bring.

A New Brand

By associating Schumacher with top-name designers, we were able to present a modern twist to the market. We carried out the most incredible launch parties too, which became a big hit for the media and press. I took out plenty of marketing for the designers in magazines, advertising, and events, which benefited them too.

These partnerships were so successful that the brand started to perk up. Soon we saw sales improve too. Suddenly, others in the industry were starting to see Schumacher in a new light.

Next, I dug into the core of the brand. I knew that over the long term, we would need someone who could create designs and displays that would wow and dazzle customers. I knew just the person I wanted to fill that role.

I reached out to Dara Caponigro, who at the time was editor-in-chief of *VERANDA* magazine. She was cool, smart, sophisticated, and all around fabulous. She was among the top editors in the interior design industry and knew everything that was going on and up-and-coming. I also was aware that the publication industry was starting to waver a bit. With that in mind, I thought it might be a great time to see if Dara wanted to come and be a creative director at Schumacher.

She'd been in publishing for her whole career, but I knew she had the best eye and that she was the one picking out everything that looked so good in the magazine. I invited her for lunch, and she thought we were going out to talk about the magazine. Of course, I was ready to use the time to work my Terri magic!

Dara agreed to meet over lunch, and when we got together, I asked her about her family and the business world she was in.

When we finished eating, I pushed back my plate and said, "I have a real thought for you, Dara. I would just love it if you would consider becoming my chief creative officer at Schumacher."

She nearly fell off her chair and hit the floor. "What?! Are you kidding me?" was all she could say. She couldn't imagine the shift to such a different role and industry.

"No, I'm not kidding," I assured her. "I have had my eyes on you for a long time. You are a talent to reckon with, and I think with you at the helm as creative director and myself as CEO, this brand is going to rock and roll."

I courted Dara for about a month, and then she said yes!

She came over to Schumacher during the third year I was with the company. She spent the first twelve months with us getting to know the brand. Then the following year, she started to make the designs fly. Under her creative eye, the company became wonderfully successful. Today, everyone's proud to have Schumacher in their home.

As I look back on those years, I'm really proud of the stamp I made at the company. After five years, I saw that I had effectively put the transformation into place. It was time for me to move on and do something different, to find another opportunity for reinvention.

Once I left, Dara stayed and continued to work her magic for the years to come. She found ways to produce exclusive products for the company and even did a book for the Schumacher brand. She oversaw new marketing campaigns and rebranded the company again. It's truly an inspiring story, brand, and company, and I was glad to be a part of it. I was able to show I could rise up and be at the top of my game again—and bring others in to follow in my steps.

Revamping a Brand

One lesson I learned during my days at Schumacher and observed at other points in my career is that changing a brand takes a significant amount of hard work, time, and innovation. I believe that all of this starts with investing in the talent of people. You need a smart, capable team, and that has a financial cost to it.

You also have to invest in marketing to get the word out. You'll want to have a great product as well. This involves getting the right people to design it and putting enough capital behind it. You'll need the right amount of financial support for the brand too.

Notice that all of these involve a form of investment. I've seen situations at companies where the financial resources were lacking, and there were key limitations on what we could do. We simply aren't able to invest in these areas if there aren't funds in place.

For this reason, when I talk to others about building and reinventing a brand, I always recommend taking some time to look at the financials. It's not enough to be told that there is money set aside. It's better to open the books and take a look and then talk as a team about how the resources should best be allocated.

Beyond the right capital, I encourage you to make sure you are creating products that you are proud to represent. As I reflect on my career, every product I worked with meant something to me. I love my portfolio and am happy to wear and display everything that I have been involved in creating.

MONITORING THE CLIENT BASE

Another critical lesson I've learned about the rebranding process is that it's best to not jump to conclusions about clients. Don't assume that all clients on record are a reflection of your company and brand. It's important to know what your customer base is like and how it may be changing. There's so much to be found in this area if you take the time to dive in, look at what's happened in the past, and consider the future.

For instance, maybe the majority of clients have been with the company for a long time. Perhaps they're getting ready to shift away from the product and try out something else, because they're moving into a different demographic that you're not targeting. Look to see who your core group of customers is. And then don't take them for granted. Existing clients might not be with you forever.

You'll also want to think about the clients that could be coming in. Which new ones are you hoping to engage with? What are they looking for? What can you offer them? Finally, think ahead to the future. Who will you be selling to in the next years? What segment of the population might be interested in your brand, and why? What solutions will you be providing for them? What will the story behind your product and company be? Make sure your sales plan covers the past, present, and future.

If you take time to look into these factors, you can lower the risk of a shrinking customer base. These are important records and metrics to track, as they lead to both current and future sales, which drive revenue. Keep in touch with your customers and know what they are looking for. You can then find ways to deliver exactly what they want and wow them in the process by providing personal, friendly service (just like Dad taught me!).

As I reflect on my journey from the shock of losing my position as CEO to the fun challenge of reinventing Schumacher, I remember that success takes a mix of hard work, creativity, and the ability to change. I leaned into new relationships and developed them to breathe new life into a company that needed to modernize. I also found ways to invest in the right talent and set a path that others could follow. I encourage you to do the same and to look at rebranding processes as an opportunity for growth and innovation.

How to Navigate Family Businesses

In many ways, working in a family business is similar to any other business, but there are some key differences. Personally, I've always been drawn to the creative, entrepreneurial spirit that runs through these environments. It's a bit like being surrounded with creative chaos—a constant flux of ideas, passion, and energy. For instance, I've worked with a designer who would sketch ideas on napkins during dinner and create masterpieces, and it was incredible to watch. I've thrived in the settings that come with family businesses, and I can set the right strategy to align a brand and drive growth.

Along the way, I've come to appreciate how deeply personal and committed family businesses can be. It isn't just a company; it's a dream for many of these families. They've invested 100 percent into making their vision a reality. They also recognize they need help with certain aspects, and that's where I come in to make magic happen and get great results.

Being Adopted into the Family

Despite the rewards, keep in mind that working in a family-owned business means that you will always be an outsider to a certain extent. The family name is their own, and you're always a step removed. But that doesn't mean you can't play an essential role. You can become a trusted advisor, a fabulous "in-law," and someone they rely on.

If you approach the situation with a mindset of courage, confidence, and collaboration, you'll be treated as one of their own. Just remember, your name may never be on the door, and that's okay. You're there to help them grow, and with a good agreement and mutual respect, you can play a vital role in the success of the business.

For someone stepping into this environment, it's like being adopted into a family—not just a business. You're entering a space built on years, if not decades, of shared experiences, traditions, and personal dedication. Whether you're stepping into a role in a small family-run business or a larger enterprise, the dynamics are often similar.

From understanding your place as an "adopted" member of the family to helping the business professionalize to finding ways to align with their passions and dreams, the following lessons can help you add your own sparkle to family-owned businesses.

Be Prepared for Family Dynamics: Family-owned businesses come with sensitivities and sometimes unexpected challenges. It's not uncommon to deal with family members who may not initially be aware of your role or what you will contribute. Tensions can arise, but they will often subside as the family sees your value.

Earn Trust by Helping: Every family business, no matter how successful, usually needs some level of professionalization. You might be able to introduce new processes, structures, or efficiencies. Look for opportunities and make change happen; they'll notice the positive improvements you make.

Understand the Financial Plan: When working for a family business, have a clear understanding of the financial incentives and how they will impact you. Are you simply an employee, or will you be considered a business partner? If you're contributing to the growth of the company, make sure you have a solid financial agreement that aligns with your efforts.

Respect Their Passion: For family business owners, their dreams, hopes, and legacy are tied up in the company. Listening carefully to what they want to achieve, along with their concerns about getting there, will help you set the right strategy. You can use your own creativity and skill to help them make a mark in the industry.

Enjoy the Ride: I've had unbelievable experiences while working for family businesses, ranging from spending time in a castle (!) to walking the red carpet and being gifted fabulous jewelry. Look for your own ways to win and have fun along the way—you might end up in amazing places you never dreamed of going.

Family businesses come with their own set of challenges, but they also offer unique rewards. If you work for one, know that you're stepping into a place where personal lives and business are intertwined. By understanding your role, earning trust, and helping the business evolve, you can create a lasting impact—even if your name isn't on the door.

Key Takeaways

- Look for ways to embrace reinvention and use it as a tool to find new opportunities.
- Never underestimate the importance of investing in top talent and strategic partnerships to breathe new life into a company.
- Monitoring and understanding your customer base are essential steps to ensure lasting relevance as a company.
- When rebranding, be open to creative new ideas, put in the extra hours, and be ready to adapt as needed to achieve success.

CHAPTER THIRTEEN

SURVIVING DESPITE ALL ODDS

After moving up through the executive ranks and reaching the CEO level and then being let go and reinventing myself to become CEO again, I started to think about my next opportunities. Certainly, I had come a long way (and I was proud of my successes!). There was still that desire to do something more or different, and I found myself becoming interested in working for a private equity firm. By this point, I had plenty of experience working with family-run companies and knew how to manage teams. I thought private equity would be a perfect next step, and I started writing letters and reaching out.

These efforts (and by that, I mean persistently pursuing firms in my nice, direct, and sassy style!) led to an offer to join Morilee, a large bridal and special occasion dress company that had been in the industry for decades and was ready to be modernized. I had never worked in the dress business, but I wasn't worried. I knew how to sell and market brands, I knew how to lead, and most of all, I knew how to make transformations happen. I was ready.

I jumped in, taking the CEO seat in 2018. I spent the first year getting to know the global company, meeting the teams and retailers, and networking with others in the industry. While I worked in the New York City office, the company had factories in China and Indonesia. I wanted to get to know every aspect of the business, so I traveled there in January and November of 2019.

During the November 2019 trip, the flight to China went well, and I had productive meetings while there. I remember when I went to the airport in Hong Kong, ready to fly home. Something in the atmosphere was changing. People were wearing masks, and there were rumors about a condition called COVID-19.

We didn't know the details of the disease or exactly the implications it would bring. I did know that COVID-19 was affecting parts of the business, as deliveries from the factories in China had slowed down. I carried on as best I could until the following spring of 2020 when the pandemic broke out in full force, and the entire world shut down.

At Morilee, we sent everyone home too. Since I wanted to avoid being in a congested area, if possible, Bart and I packed up our apartment in New York City and went to our house in East Hampton, New York. The place had previously served as our weekend home, and it quickly became our permanent residence. I felt it would be safer to be more isolated, and I checked on my loved ones regularly to see how they were doing and make sure they were taking protective measures too.

As I sat there surveying what our society was now facing, I wondered along with the rest of the world: How will we get through this, personally and professionally? As CEO of Morilee, I felt an extra responsibility to take care of the staff and team members. Soon I was at my computer every day at 5:00 a.m., searching vigorously for ways to keep the global company alive, help the employees morally and financially, and get everyone through the crisis and to the other side.

Financial Decisions

Picture this for a moment: you're in the wedding and special occasion dress business, and your ability to generate revenue depends on the sale of dresses. Then all weddings and events are suddenly postponed until … a further date. In the meantime, you know that consumers will not be buying special attire to wear when going out, because they are all staying home.

That's exactly what I faced during 2020 as I oversaw a company that wouldn't be making sales to retailers in the short term. We had more than three thousand stores globally that ordered from us during pre-pandemic times. But with COVID-19 racing across the planet, there was really no reason for retailers to buy dresses.

I also was aware that retailers would be struggling as their stores were closed to the public and the demand for their merchandise plummeted. All the forecasts for the year which had been made pre-COVID-19 were no longer relevant. The world had changed, and the whole wedding industry took a large hit as well as numerous other businesses, as we know. For our part, with the shutdown, our business evaporated.

With that in mind, the first step I took as CEO during COVID-19 was to ask, "Do we have enough cash?" I knew that we had a lot of mouths to feed globally. We had a workforce around the world, and they would be depending on the company to keep paying them.

I checked what was in the company account and what we were owed. Prior to reaching this point, I had tended to pay more attention to the front of the house, focusing on sales and marketing. I liked to follow the orders as they were entered into the system. With the crisis underway, I had to know how the back of the house was holding up, where cash came in as retailers paid off their accounts and collections were made.

It was a huge lesson for me. I saw that, fortunately, we had a fair amount of cash. However, we were owed way too much for us to be comfortable for long. My heart dropped as I scanned the numbers. They made the company appear like a bank to the retailers, because there was so much due that hadn't come in. *How am I going to get these payments to come through?* I wondered. The retailers had closed their doors. How were they going to be able to pay us what they owed?

Still, we couldn't carry on without collecting at least some of the payments. We would have to use a strategy to get our cash up so that payroll would continue. Like always, I knew it would be largely based on relationships. I would need to work with my team and our retail customers to learn about their needs and find a path forward so we wouldn't have to let people go or close our business permanently.

CONNECTING IN NEW WAYS

For every business that I've operated in, I've always considered those that work for me to be my family. During COVID-19, I knew that our staff was hunkered down and that the loneliness and fear factors were high. I felt I needed to have a presence and keep everyone going.

Thanks to Zoom, I could gather our staff and management online weekly and talk daily during COVID-19. This meant that I met with about one hundred people on a call once a week. I took it upon myself to keep the momentum going and the vibe positive. I saw myself as the mom of the family and wanted to check on everybody. I got dressed up every day and made sure I looked nice, just as I always had during my career. I learned how to present well on Zoom too, as I knew it would be a main way to communicate during the months ahead.

I also met with the sales team on their own once every week to go over progress and make sure everybody was okay. These individuals were at a loss, as they knew we wouldn't be able to sell anything. Surely, they were wondering what would happen to their job if they could get orders.

I advised them to just stay in touch with retailers. "Don't call and ask for an order—that would be offensive," I said. "We don't know if this will last for six months or a year or longer, but for now, you can listen to customers. They might be scared out of their minds right now."

And that's precisely what we did. The salespeople started calling the retailers, and rather than trying to make a sale, they asked how everything was going at the stores. Then we would meet as a team once a week and talk about who we had called. We would share the information we had gathered from the retailers. Through these conversations, we learned that the stores basically had no business.

PROVIDING INCENTIVES

Even though I could understand the situation our retailers were in, I also knew that our company needed funds to carry on. I decided to offer a special incentive to struggling retailers for paying invoices promptly. It certainly improved company cash flow during the COVID crisis. I thought, *I need an incentive to pull the cash from the retailers*. I wanted to give a discount which would be helpful to them and allow them to pay off some of their accounts. We agreed that we could provide a 2 percent cash discount to the bills that we were owed.

For some of the larger stores, this discount was seen as a good benefit. They paid their bills, and that gave the company bank account a boost. Soon it was at a much better level than it had been in the past.

Coping Mechanisms

As the months rolled on and we entered the summer of 2020, I realized that the luster of working from home was wearing off for many people. I personally was tired of figuring out how to manage each day. It was challenging to try and think that life would be okay again too.

During this time, I also had to meet every week with lenders and explain to them what the company was going through. I had to show them a PowerPoint to explain what we were doing and why. I would assure them that weddings were postponed but not canceled. I was repeating the same information week after week, and there was no end in sight.

Eventually, as the finances continued to remain down due to the crisis, I knew we wouldn't be able to maintain payroll. We would have to make a change in salary or start reducing the number of staff members. I didn't want to cut anybody, so instead, I came up with a different solution. I met with the team and asked them to take a pay cut. I shared with them that I simply couldn't continue to pay them the same levels of salary with no business.

"I need help," I explained. "I'm going to do my best to get it back." In reality, I honestly didn't know if I would ever be able to return salaries to the same level they were at prior to the pandemic. Everyone agreed to take a cut, and we reduced salaries by an average of 20 percent for the next months. I knew the amount was significant and that team members would notice the reduced income. Still, it greatly helped with our payroll situation.

I also took measures to make other cuts where I could. I had to place a hold on paying rent for our office, as we weren't even using the space we were leasing with everyone working at home. I knew I would be able to send over enough for the rent payments we missed once business picked up again. In the meantime, I felt it was important to prioritize our people and give them as much as we could to support them and the people who were depending on them to bring home a paycheck.

Finding a Coach

One morning in July of 2020, I sat outside on the back patio of our lovely East Hampton home. I held a little cup of fresh coffee in my hand, and I sipped it while reading through the *New York Times*. I turned to the business section, and a headline caught my attention. I read, "If You're a CEO through COVID-19, Hire Yourself a Coach."

It sounded interesting, and my eyes turned to the full text below the title. The article discussed how the age-old notion of it being lonely at the top had taken on a whole new meaning with the pandemic. It encouraged individuals who had reached a high professional level in their career to consider getting a coach.

The message really hit home for me. There I was, working so hard every day to help the company survive. I wanted to care for our employees and also manage our retail customers in the right way as we all navigated the crises before us. How could I plan out a future when I didn't know what the next day would bring? What more could I do to help the company and our people? Who could I turn to for advice on next steps? Who would be able to relate to my situation and provide valuable insight?

As soon as I finished reading the article, I knew that I needed a coach. I searched for one and found a business expert specializing in helping CEOs through COVID-19 that I could call up. We held sessions that were incredibly meaningful for me both personally and professionally. I could talk to this person as a business partner and ask for his perspective on what I was going through. I learned that he too had been through interesting experiences and was very knowledgeable about best business practices.

(Looking back on this, I have to laugh a bit—it's funny to me to think that at the time, none of us knew anything about COVID-19. How could a person become a "COVID-19 expert" for businesses when it was impossible to know what would happen next? Though I give my coach, David Kaplowitz, credit because he knew how to handle a crisis, and he shared great insights with me.)

For me, the chance to talk about the challenges I was facing was very helpful. I could share what was going on and then work with the coach to find solutions. It enabled me to make decisions that I knew would be good for the company and also important to our team members.

The Party Continues

My love for throwing a good party didn't end with COVID-19. Even though we were all inside our homes, logging into work from our laptops, I knew we could find ways to have fun and celebrate. I started googling for good ideas on Zoom parties and events and set up some memorable events that helped lift everyone's mood.

I came up with something creative we could do every week during our global team call. Once, we followed a theme called "The Best Cocktail." Even though we were spread out, I assured everyone it was five o'clock somewhere. We all brought our favorite recipe and held up our cocktail. For the following weeks, I came up with a new theme for every meeting. We also recognized birthdays and celebrated special occasions over Zoom as a group.

These regular meetings, along with the continuing relationships with retailers, really kept us going through COVID-19. Our team members pulled together like a family and held on to each other. The retailers appreciated the care and compassion we showed them and how confident we were that we would get through the pandemic.

New In-Store Offerings

Thanks to my ongoing dedication and commitment to the company, along with my helpful coaching sessions, I came up with some great ideas to move our business forward and help retailers get a strong start once COVID-19 passed. One of these involved the launching of an in-store Morilee bridal dress boutique.

I thought it would be wonderful if brides could walk into a retailer and have a special spot where they could be dazzled with fresh furniture and fun displays, like a video monitor featuring them in a runway-style way. I wanted them to be delighted with dresses in their size, just waiting to be tried on. The whole concept would sparkle and shine and bring customers bursting through the doors of retailers as soon as they had the chance.

I knew it would be the perfect way to reinvent the industry. It would be a fabulous look for our business once we passed through the pandemic. Retailers could have something to look forward to and a reason to invite customers into their stores. These shops could have the chance to have higher sales, which would translate to more orders for our company. And brides would have an amazing experience picking out their dress and making their dreams come true.

To put my idea into motion, I started calling up retailers to share my thoughts with them. I knew that I would have to work through several barriers. One of these was the fact that I was seen as a newbie to the bridal industry. I had built a name for myself in other segments, including cosmetics, jewelry, and home furnishings. But surely, many would be questioning what I could possibly know about the dress business, as I had only been involved in it for about one and a half years at that point.

I would also have to work through the issue that we didn't know when the pandemic would end. If stores thought that there would never be a chance to operate as they had before, they wouldn't be as motivated to provide something for future customers. I knew that some of the locations were probably ready for a makeover or some touch-ups like fresh paint. There wouldn't be an incentive to invest in a store's look unless a picture for brighter and better times could be painted.

There would also be a question of how it could be done and what the store might look like. For that, I turned to a talented woodworker I knew named Ray. He had done some beautiful cabinetry work that I admired in my apartment building. I was convinced he would be perfect to carry out the look I wanted, which included furniture, a runway with a video monitor, and dresses hung in a new way. I wanted some of the dresses to be front-facing in several spots rather than all sideways on a rack.

Ray lived in Upstate New York, where he ran a little shop with a few craftsmen. I called him up and told him, "Put on a mask. I want to meet and share my vision with you." When I explained the concept to Ray, he agreed. I wanted every boutique to look the same so that they would all align with the Morilee branding. I knew it would have to be of high quality, to look like it was first-class. Together Ray and I came up with a beautiful design that could be built. He would travel to the stores and create the boutiques with his crew.

To overcome the concerns that I knew retailers would have, I crafted my message in a positive, confident way that showed I cared about their stores and customers. I set up Zoom meetings so we could discuss the project and what it would look like. When I talked to the owners and managers of the retail stores, I introduced myself first in a kind, even tone.

"Hello! I'm Terri Eagle," I began. "I'm the new CEO of Morilee, and I want to speak with you. I've seen that you're a top-performing bridal account. Thank you for your business. I have worked in a few industries, and one of the ideas I carried out at David Yurman was to launch a boutique in-store concept."

The person on the other end always asked what that might be like, so I would explain my idea. I had pictures of the concept too that I shared with them.

I told the retailers how the in-store boutiques could be marketed and how the video monitor would be placed. They would be placed inside locations that were our clients. There would be a special built-in section for Morilee, and it would feel like its own setting. It would have dresses that brides could try on in many sizes and selections, model for their try-on, and enjoy the experience. After I told them about it, a lot of stores decided to paint, to redo their interiors, or to carry out other upgrades. They made changes that really made the interiors sparkle—just as I envisioned.

I worked closely with my national sales manager, Suly, throughout the project to get everything in place. We agreed with the stores that we would build the furniture for the boutiques and ship it to their store. The retailers, in turn, bought dresses to place in the boutiques, and they put in orders for more sizes so that brides could try on the dresses right in the shop. In less than two years, we had placed in-store boutiques in thirty-five locations, and the sales growth was significant!

THE AMBASSADOR PROGRAM

With the top bridal shops that we sold to, I wanted to create marketing strategies that would both help and motivate them to sell more. I set up an ambassador program that could be launched right when COVID-19 ended. Its design was to incentivize stores to sell our brand, and the better they did, the more they made on a monthly bonus check. More than thirty-five bridal retailers decided to participate, and it turned into a real powerhouse for the business.

When 2022 came to an end, we had carried out the best sales year the company had ever had. In reflection, I owe much of it to our great team and also to the retailers who said yes! COVID-19 taught me to think ahead and to pursue as many social engagements as I could after the pandemic ended.

Because of the great business outcome after COVID-19, we were able to pay the team back the pay cut they had taken. I saved enough and put the amount that had been taken out in their end-of-the-year check. Their holidays arrived with an amount they never expected, equivalent to what had been deducted from their salary during COVID-19.

I had been right all along—weddings had only been postponed. After COVID-19, the events came back on the calendar, and customers started walking into the stores again. When they did, they were welcomed with fabulous in-store bridal boutiques. Their delight was so high that they quickly tried on dresses and found the ones that made them feel special and beautiful.

Besides the survival of the business during COVID-19, I had another great takeaway from the shutdown. It made me realize just how important face-to-face meetings are, and you'll now regularly find me calling people I haven't talked to in a while and meeting up with girlfriends more consistently than I did prior to COVID-19. These days, I love making time for the special people in my life, including my doggies, my husband, and my friends.

Let's toast to that.

THE BENEFITS OF SURVIVING

Despite the many unexpected challenges of COVID-19, especially being in the bridal and special occasion dress industry, I was able to navigate Morilee through the storm by focusing on cash flow, supporting my team, and staying connected with our retailers. The pandemic forced me to reimagine how we operated, and those efforts ultimately paid off. From launching in-store boutiques to creating an ambassador program, we not only survived, but also came out stronger. The experience reinforced the importance of courage, confidence, and collaboration to solve problems. Through it all, I've learned to celebrate both the small wins and the big ones—and to always keep moving forward, ready to face what's ahead.

Key Takeaways

- Navigating the challenges of COVID-19 required a commitment to keep the business going and a dedication to team members to support them as well. Put a smile on despite the odds!
- The ability to simply listen to customers and provide empathy, rather than try to sell more to them, helped improve our relationships with them. They saw us as a key partner and turned to us when events came back on the calendar.
- For a CEO, the right coach can provide invaluable support and insight and offer a perspective that helps you make strategic decisions for the future.
- As you go through life's ups and downs, be sure to take time for yourself and your loved ones. Schedule regular meetups with friends so you can stay connected and in tune with each other's lives.

PART FIVE

CARE

CHAPTER FOURTEEN

THE VELVET HAMMER

If you come and visit me in my office today, you'll find I keep a beautiful wooden, custom-engraved box on display. It has my name, Terri, carved into the covering in lovely lettering. At first glance, you might think it's a desk set, as it's about the size to hold a few pens and stationery.

However, when you open it, you'll quickly see that inside, resting on black velvet lining, is a hammer. It features the words, "The Velvet Hammer," followed with the description: "You are direct and impactful yet lead with innate diplomacy, compassion, and warmth."

My CFO Deborah Klemm gave me the gift, and the phrase "the velvet hammer" has been an ongoing joke between colleagues and myself for years. While I love to treat everyone with kindness and respect, as was instilled in me during my early years, I also recognize that we need to get things done. To me, the nicely packaged hammer in my office is a reminder that it's possible to send a direct message with a soft touch.

I have found over the years that this type of leadership style works wonders! You can get great deals, negotiate in a professional way, and best of all, create positive results. It is also a helpful strategy to maintain relationships, as it helps you stay focused on the people involved.

Picking Up the Title

The first time someone ever mentioned the phrase "velvet hammer" to me, I was in the process of negotiating with the GQ Men of the Year Awards and *Vogue* magazine. I wanted to take out some pages for advertising and had contacted an executive, Tom Florio, to discuss the opportunity. I was working to be friendly while also pushing for the spread I wanted. I knew I needed something special to promote the brand and company.

I was with David Yurman at the time, and we were trying to secure pages that were usually dedicated to large cosmetic and car companies. If I wasn't pushy, we would never have landed them, as the magazine publisher would have simply stayed with the traditional contracts.

Tom recognized my persistence, and at one point, he simply said, "Okay, just get your velvet hammer out." He went on to explain, "Around here, we call you The Velvet Hammer, because you have a nice and little sassy but firm way of getting things done." And guess what? I got the pages I wanted!

While that was about the first time in my career that someone pointed out I operated with a velvet hammer, I have used these methods for a long time. They're simply effective and help you accomplish tasks while maintaining a smile. In fact, I love to negotiate with this style for just about everything in life, both personally and professionally.

THE THRILL OF THE CHASE

Wherever you go, you'll see that everything has a price. And there's often a better option available—if you can just find it and get others to agree to it. If you make a reservation at a restaurant, how do you know if you're getting the perfect spot for the best price? When you're buying a car, how can you be assured you'll be given the best option available for the most suitable price in your budget? You simply have to ask—and you have to know how to approach the questions.

I travel frequently for work and have been in many different hotel rooms over the years. The reservation that I often have is for a nice room, but not the top one. I negotiate by just asking a question, which can lead to a better room that the establishment has to offer.

When I arrive at the hotel where I'll be staying, I often start by approaching the receptionist behind the counter and checking their name tag. I greet them by name and ask how their day is going. Then I explain that I travel so much and would appreciate having a really nice room. I'll ask if there is an upgrade available, or a space with a better view that I might be able to take instead of the room assigned to me.

As the conversation about possible hotel rooms unfolds, I keep a friendly demeanor. I love to be a little funny and clever but to keep kindness at the heart of every discussion. I just about always get a better room and other perks that aren't readily available.

Teaching Others

For a recent event I held for retailers who were coming from out of town to New York City, I wanted to give them an amazing evening, one that would make them feel special and really dazzle them. It took me some time to decide on the perfect approach that would be practical for a Tuesday night, which was when I planned to take them out during their stay.

On the Saturday prior to the event, I found exactly what I wanted—it was a yacht from 1927, built in Paris. We could take it out for the evening and have a dinner on the water. It would be perfect for the group of thirty-five people we would be entertaining, which were key retail bridal partners. We could toast to our teams there and together celebrate our partnerships.

There was just one problem. The price the company was asking to rent it for an evening was higher than my budget. Rather than search for other options or give up, I put my negotiation skills and velvet hammer to work. I had my associate business manager working with me, and she would be the one having discussions about the rental. I would need to prepare her and help her feel equipped to carry a conversation about the yacht and get it for a price that was within our budget. This would mean getting the company to drop their price by nearly 50 percent of the starting figure.

I formed a strategy and then explained it. "First, you call up the company and say, 'I'm working with my CEO, and I'm the business associate manager. She has her heart set on this yacht, and I really want to make it happen for her. I saw you have great reviews, and she only wants to book with you."

The manager with the company overseeing the yacht would likely respond that it would cost $20,000 for our group of nearly thirty-five people. I requested her to continue by saying, "Oh, this is really sad, as that's not in our budget. But my CEO thinks you might be able to—since it seems like it's still available, and our event is in just a couple of days—give us a price of $10,000."

The manager went for it! And the yacht was absolutely gorgeous. On Tuesday evening, the retailers walked aboard a vessel that was so well decorated that it looked magical. We had a cocktail hour, served dinner, and listened to a three-piece jazz band. The evening was so special. And it only cost about half of the starting price!

USING THE VELVET HAMMER WISELY

As I look back on these times, I think of the occasions that I have pulled out the velvet hammer (or encouraged others to do so). It creates a way to maintain and build relationships while also working to find a solution. Rather than point fingers at other people, you can invite them to join in the process and remind them of what needs to be done. After all, hitting goals while still being kind is a skill that can get you places—and it will make you and your team feel happy about what you've accomplished together.

Key Takeaways

- Use the Velvet Hammer leadership style by blending directness with diplomacy and compassion to achieve results while maintaining strong relationships.
- Negotiating with persistence and kindness can help you explain your situation and get the best outcome possible.
- When others come to you for advice, encourage them to drive positive change while treating team members and customers with respect.
- Once you've mastered a balance of firmness and warmth in your leadership position, you'll find that you can go further than you ever imagined. That's what I did! I continue to think it's one of the best strategies for leading a company and achieving high levels of success.

CHAPTER FIFTEEN

A REASON TO CELEBRATE

Not long ago, I had a COO who went on vacation to Florence, Italy. When he arrived at the hotel he was staying at for the trip, he walked into his room and found a bottle of champagne. It was ready and waiting for him, a little extra indulgence for his well-deserved break. And the card with it ended, "Thank you! Enjoy! XOXO, Terri."

I wanted to send an extra treat for his vacation. Everyone gets a little something from me for their birthday, a special occasion, their getaway trips, or any event that is worth a celebration. It's part of my approach to being a Champagne CEO.

That's what business—and life—really is about in many ways. Yes, we go through challenges, and there are plenty of hard times. We also form relationships with people in our work and personal lives who play a key role in who we are and the successes we have. Together we can work hard and do great things. And along the way, I love to shower people with praise, kindness, and surprises that sparkle to let them know just how much they are appreciated.

A Reason to Stay

Building a great team takes a significant investment of time. And to work toward a goal, you need a pool of talent. Once I've placed people in the right positions, I help them find ways to grow and develop further. I look for their input and make decisions with them. We rise together as a team and set aside time collectively to celebrate our wins and toast to how far we have come together.

As part of this arrangement, there are little touches that I like to do throughout the year. I want people to feel like they are in a place that is much more than a career for me. I don't want them to feel like they have to work or are burdened by their tasks. I prefer them to be happy and fulfilled.

This means I make sure they take time off and enjoy the days that they are away. I will often ask before someone goes on vacation to find out what they're doing. When it's the birthday of a staff member, I always make sure a gift box is sent to them during their birthday month. If they're heading away, I find ways to create an element of surprise at their hotel upon arrival. It's so fun to give them a little thoughtful appreciation when they land.

THE VALUE IN BREAKS

Every day, I work to have balance in all that I do. I want to live my life to the fullest, both personally and professionally. I think a lot of CEOs, myself included, think we can do it all. It's so easy to avoid taking breaks or going on vacation. Yet I have found that time away is invaluable—it is essential for success.

I regularly set aside time to take vacations, and I check out when I can. I try to do this well so that my team has an example to follow. For instance, Bart and I try to go to Anguilla in the Caribbean every

February. It's the most peaceful place and has beautiful beaches. I use the time there to step back and dive into a good book. We also take walks, play tennis, and enjoy the sunshine and water.

Bart and I also pursue our love of biking, and that takes us on adventures around the world. We're highly dedicated to Backroads, a company specializing in luxury cycling activities, and they do the most incredible trips. We've been to so many countries and even did a trip in my home state of Washington.

These trips include traveling with others, usually about twenty to twenty-five, and exploring, cycling, and eating together—it's a bit like camp! I'll admit I was nervous when we first started backroads trips. I remember going to camp when I was ten years old. I didn't enjoy sleeping in makeshift places, and I missed being home. I flunked camp as a kid and wanted to go back home sooner than later.

You can imagine my concerns when we first took trips with other adults through Backroads. For our first Backroads trip, Bart and I biked in the Loire Valley in France for my fortieth birthday. It was fabulous. We realized we enjoyed being with groups of all ages and going to amazing places together.

For the trip, we would have breakfast and then bike for between twenty and thirty miles a day. We all had maps and could bike together or on our own. In the morning, there would be a stopping point along the way to see something spectacular. Then we would eat a picnic lunch or stop in a gorgeous village to eat—and the meal was always accompanied by a glass of wine. After that, we would be back on the bike, and we would also come across other sites and markets to shop at.

A backup van for support followed, so if you grew tired of biking, you could catch a ride. They also gave us snack packs (my favorite were the peanut M&M'S!) and water bottles, so we really had everything we needed and more. By midafternoon, the route would end at a luxury hotel. There, we could relax, get a massage, or walk around and see the area. Some nights, we ate individually, and others, we joined for a group meal.

Over the years, we have gone to so many off-the-beaten-path places and seen the best sights. It's been a magical experience, and I have loved being a part of it. Bart and I usually extend the trip and take a couple of extra days to enjoy a nearby place, making the most of our travel and experience.

In addition to vacations, I believe that for those in senior management positions, it can be healthy to do something every quarter as a mini celebration. It could be an extended weekend, such as taking a Friday off and returning the following Monday. As a Champagne CEO, I do that and highly recommend it. Boy, that does feel good!

Ongoing Care

I like to take measures for clients that are appropriate for when we meet up at conferences, meetings, and other occasions. At a recent event, I gave everyone in attendance a bag which held a beautiful Glassybaby candle. It had a little tea light inside and a nice message with it. Inside the bags were also darling heart-shaped sunglasses. The idea was, "Put your shades on, because the collections are going to be so fabulous and bright."

Whenever there is a funeral or one of our team member's family members passes away, I always have the company cater the lunch after the service. I really take pride in doing that, as it's a way to show we care and to celebrate the life of their loved one.

Everyday Energy

I work so hard to take care of the company and our staff that my team often teases me. They say I act like the Energizer Bunny, because I'm always up early and ready to jump into the day. It's true that business and work are important to me and that I love to get things done. That said, I've also found ways to slow down a bit and appreciate the moment—even if that means I'm not answering emails immediately.

One of the triggers that changed this all-out driven habit I had acquired came in the form of my new fur baby. This little puppy, Kazzy, was so demanding as a puppy and really a wild fur baby! She really didn't sleep that much, and she wanted to play all the time. She would wake up at 5:00 a.m. and insist on getting attention. I would get up and take her for a walk (I really had no other choice!). She's such a social butterfly and would want to greet her little friends and watch the birds for so long that we would return home about forty-five minutes later.

At first, I would feel the rush to get back home and check my emails. But after a while, as I watched her gaze at the sky, be fascinated with squirrels, and simply love life, I started to care less about the urgency of the day's business prior to 6:00 a.m.! It really was the best medicine ever, and it truly changed course for me. I wanted to take care of her, and in doing so, I started taking better care of myself (and fortunately, the puppy started sleeping until 6:00 a.m. most days!).

These days, I look forward to getting up with her and taking her out for a walk in NYC. I also head out with her at night after work, and it's a great way to unwind and relax. She helps me see the beauty in our neighborhood and to remember that stepping away from work can help me be more productive when I'm back to my laptop and phone.

Going through the Hard Times

When I joined Morilee as CEO, I was brought in to professionalize and modernize and grow the business to the next level. The team members, under my supervision, had gone through plenty of ups and downs together. One of the recent challenges we had to get through started when the lead designer of the company resigned.

She had been with the company for forty years and stepped away at a key time for us. We needed about nine hundred new sketches for our upcoming collections in less than two months' time. As a leader in the bridal and special occasion dress business, you can imagine the gap that was left.

That said, I knew what to do immediately, and I lined up a top executive search firm to help fill the position. I was confident the company would be able to help me find a great designer, and I launched the search soon after she resigned. Suddenly, we had a lot of extra work on our hands.

I also reached out to our team and looked for what we could do. I knew we had two top designers who had been working under the lead designer that left. Would they be willing to stay and step up? We had to carry out a big design project in a short amount of time, and I didn't know who would be up for the challenge.

I started by calling the two top Morilee designers into my office. "Ladies," I said. "We have five dress divisions, and we need designs for each of them. I have a good feeling about you, and I think you can do it. But right now, it's not about me—it's about you. I want you to leave the office and take a couple of days to think about it. If you want to step away, I only ask that you give me about a six-week notice, just so we can carry on. But I know you both have great talent, and I think that together we can figure it out. Go ahead and take a couple of days, and then give me your answer if you want to stay or if you'll be moving on in six weeks."

The two nodded and left my office. We needed to accomplish a lot in six weeks. I assured the ownership I could handle the situation and to give me time.

Two days later, the two top designers came back. They walked into my office unannounced.

"Hi ladies!" I said. "Sit down, and let's talk."

They explained to me that they wanted to stay and get the job done. They had just one condition: they asked that the assistant designer who worked at the company be promoted so she could help out with the project.

I readily agreed. I gave all three of them immediate promotions!

Then we got to work. I explained that we needed to present the new lines of dresses to retailers in ten weeks. I assured them I would help them organize a schedule and prioritize to get everything done. I would also role-play with them so they knew what to say when they presented the dresses. It was a Wednesday, and I said we would meet the following Monday to have a roundtable and lay out a plan.

When Monday came, they walked into my office again. This time, they looked incredibly scared. I quickly met with them and asked what was wrong. "Terri," they said, "There are nine hundred designs that we have to complete in four weeks. It's a lot."

I knew it was a huge task. I said, "We have a lot of work ahead of us. Let's look at what we have to do. We have five lines—bridal, quinceañera, bridesmaid, special occasion, and prom. And we need nine hundred sketches in all. Let's look at the most important business first. And let's lay out a story for each line."

That's exactly what we did. We broke down the project by weeks. We filled in what had to be done for each line and when we would get it completed.

During the days that followed, the designers worked hard and met their deadlines. They even traveled to the factories that produced the dresses so they could meet with the team members in those locations. By the time ten weeks were up, they had all the sketches done, and everything was ready to present to our clients.

The grand finale took place in New York City, when we showed a preview of our new collections to our top retailers. When the retailers came and saw what the designers had done, they loved the new dresses! The pieces were so modern and fresh, and the designers presented everything very professionally.

After the show, we took everyone to a dinner. There were about forty people in attendance, and I was hosting a table with some of our key partners. Right before dessert was served, I was called away from my table. I was told that one of the top designers wanted me at the bar.

I went over quickly, worried that the designers were maybe not okay. I knew I had asked them to do so much work in a short time and with a lot of pressure. When I got up to the bar, I saw the two top designers—and three martinis. They handed me one of them and said, "Terri, we just want to say thank you, because you believed in us when we didn't believe in ourselves." They toasted me and said, "We didn't know what we didn't know. And you saw it. So thank you again."

I said, "Ladies, thank you! You did it! Congrats!"

BRING ON THE SPARKLE

In the end, I found a new chief design officer and brought her on to build out the design team. From the day I walked into that door six years ago, I did not take my eye off the ball. It wasn't easy, but I didn't give up for my team.

At my last sales and marketing meeting, a team member turned to me and added, "Terri, they need to know what they don't know, because they don't live with you every day, and I watch what goes on in your life, and it's remarkable what you get done on a daily basis to make this company move."

When she finished, everyone cheered. And then they said, "Terri, we need the champagne to toast you! Our fearless leader!"

In the end, leadership isn't just about hard work; it's about celebrating the journey, the people, and the successes that happen along the way. Whether it's sending a bottle of champagne to show someone you are thinking of them, investing in your team's growth and capabilities, or simply finding joy in life's everyday moments, the Champagne CEO mindset is about balance, care, and appreciation. As we move forward, we grow stronger together—overcoming challenges, inspiring each other to go for the next goal, and always finding a reason to raise a glass to the sparkle we create as a team.

Key Takeaways

- Consider incorporating thoughtful gestures, such as personalized gifts and special touches, to let your team members know you care for them and their well-being.
- When you look to recruit other team members, give them a taste of what they will experience when they work with you–and make it so special that they want to come over as soon as possible and stay!

- Every business undergoes challenging times at some point. If you surround yourself with a great team, you can manage the situation together and collectively put in extra hours to get to a better place.
- Don't fear setbacks, as they are a way to build up others and strengthen what you already have.
- Celebrate small and large wins, and always be ready to shower praise on others. By developing people, you're contributing to their happiness and the future of the company. If you look for it, you can always find something positive to highlight.

CONCLUSION

In my life and work, as others reflect on the path I've led and how far I've come, rising from the ground up to the CEO level, I hope that they see—as I do—that the hard work to get here is worthwhile. I want to leave a legacy of love for others to see, as I have, the value in caring for your brand and your team. During the hard times, I know how to mix up a great lemonade. And as the Champagne CEO, I'm the first one to celebrate each and every success. I have created partnerships along the way by building up relationships, and I've had the great fortune of working with amazing people.

When others ask me about their own retirement, I advise looking for ways to build a legacy as part of the succession planning. As a CEO, I recognize that the job requires an ability to multitask, to prioritize, to make key decisions, and to be able to be a change-maker. Ultimately, you are always accountable and responsible for the company. I encourage you to use the traits I have—courage, confidence, and collaboration—to find your own way and leave a path for others to follow.

Courage

Throughout my career, I've always been someone who looks for ways to win and takes on challenges with an optimistic approach. I've faced the uncertainty that comes with leadership and worked hard to make everything come together as brands rebuild and then skyrocket. Courage has been key—pushing through tough times, learning to adapt, and overcoming obstacles to keep moving forward. I hope my journey shows others that rising to the top does include hard knocks, but the effort is absolutely worth it in the end.

Confidence

I've learned to trust not only myself, but also the incredible teams I've built time and again. Being surrounded by strong, capable staff members gives me confidence in facing any problem that comes our way. As a CEO, you must make hard decisions, and I've always known that looking out for my team is number one. With the right support system and training in place, you can turn to others to step up when needed, which will you allow to pass the baton when you're ready to take on your next adventure. Confidence in people and teamwork will take your leadership to the next level. And having the confidence in yourself to ask for the next opportunity in your career—a position, promotion, or compensation—will help you go far. You have nothing to lose and everything to gain! Just ASK!

Collaboration

Building lasting partnerships has been essential throughout my career. I've had the fortune of working with amazing individuals and fostering relationships that have helped propel companies and brands forward. Listening to input from everyone around me has brought invaluable perspectives, shaping my leadership approach. I make it a priority to connect with people—whether it's lunch, dinner, or informal meetups—because those relationships often lead to future opportunities and deeper collaborations.

The Champagne CEO

As I reflect on my journey from the ground up to CEO, I think about the milestones and the joy of each achievement. I'm known for celebrating victories, no matter how small. While the road can be tough, especially at the top where leadership can feel lonely, I find strength in remembering the people who've supported me—especially my family, friends, and colleagues. They've helped me turn challenges into great outcomes and have been there for every champagne-worthy moment. At the end of the day, life is full of opportunities to reinvent yourself, and I wake up every day excited for what lies ahead, ready to toast to the next success.

Finding someone you trust to fill that position can be tough, but if you have great people and provide the training they need to move up, you'll be better equipped to take the risk and pass the baton.

With that in mind, I want to share some of the most inspiring business leaders, friends, and mentors in my life. You'll find past, present, and rising stars in the following list:

The Men in My Life:

- My dad, Bill: Forever in my heart.
- My hubby, Bart: Thirty-five-plus years of love, support, and fun.

- Lou Cona: Twenty-plus years of a treasured special friendship and business partnerships.
- Stanislas de Quercize: Number one career mentor.
- David Yurman: Most inspiring design legend.
- Michael Gould: Number one career business partner and friend.
- KX: Forever friend and advisor.
- Alan Dubow: Great fun and a caring friend for over thirty years!
- Timothy Corrigan: My forever friend.
- Steven Blechman: Inspiring and smart business leader and dear friend.

The Ladies in My Life:

- My mom, Neva: The most positive lady with a heart of gold.
- My bestie, Lael Paul: Fifty-plus years of a treasured and fabulous friendship.
- Michelle Levine: My first NYC L'Oréal and The Fragrance Group work bestie and my dear friend for over thirty years!
- Amy R. Churgin: Twenty-five-plus years of friendship and business partnership.
- Marnie McBryde: Twenty-five-plus years of special friendship, business partnership, and coaching.
- Donna Cona: Twenty-plus years, a true, forever, caring friend.
- Susan Pomerantz and Debbie Miller: Forever friends of thirty-plus years.

- Claire Gilvar: Twenty-five plus years of work and friendship—bestie!
- Deborah Klemm: Best memories building three businesses together.
- Sybil Yurman: Cheers to a brilliant marketer and branding guru!
- Surim Campos: Forever friend, businesswoman, and marketing maven!
- Suly Yu: Fabulous friend and businesswoman.
- Rachel Hartman: A new fabulous friend and inspiring, lovely, and smart woman.
- Molly Kuffner: Twenty-plus years friend and great businesswoman.
- Jenefer Lass: Number one mentor.

Rising Stars in My Life:

- Ethan Paul: Vanderbilt MBA 2024, Vanderbilt baseball star, pro-baseball star, Vanderbilt executive manager 2024, and future CEO!
- Lili Blechman: Shining star!
- Lauren Steffes: Number one lady of inspiring leadership.

Best Doggies in My Life During Thirty-Plus Years:

- Nikki, the Bichon: Sixteen-plus years (the first puppy for Bart and I together and Bart's first dog ever).
- Zoe, the Bichon: Twelve-plus years (sweetest pup ever).

- Kazzy the Cavachon: Born December 27, 2022. Ever since she joined us, it's been pure puppy bliss! Toys, squirrels, and birds are her life's simple pleasures!

As I look both back and ahead, I can't help but think of my dad's teachings to always be kind and good. Rather than be hard on yourself, look for ways to take care of yourself. Also look for ways to shower love on your family and friends, which I like to call the daily dose of love. Did you call your friend? Did you say goodbye when your loved one left? Finally, look after your team and business, and take the time to care for them too. Celebrate their milestones, gift them surprises, remember their special days, and be there for them when they are going through hard times. Surround yourself with a great group of people, celebrate them, mentor them, acknowledge and listen to them, and together, you will drive success, professionally and personally.

As a young person, I admired and respected my father's heart and soul, his goodness, his risk-taking, his dedication, and his love for his family. He had such incredible qualities, and he didn't have it easy. He grew up in the Depression era and always believed in saving money. He worked so hard and never gave up. He continued on his journey and pushed forward, and he ended up doing very well. He taught me how to act in my personal and professional life, and I will always be grateful for that.

As I think about where I am today, I am continually reminded that the deepest, dearest love of my life is my dad. Forever in my mind, heart, and soul.

Love,

Terri

ABOUT THE AUTHOR

Terri Eagle is a visionary global business executive with over twenty-five years of transformative leadership in corporate, private, family, and private equity-owned ventures. Known for her strategic insight and innovative spirit, Terri has driven profitable growth, launched groundbreaking brands, and revitalized legacy names across diverse sectors, including cosmetics, fragrance, jewelry, home decor, home interior design, and fashion.

Throughout her career, Terri has excelled at building dynamic teams and fostering strong client relationships—skills that have consistently fueled her success. She specializes in combining strategic foresight with creative innovation, positioning brands for long-term growth and pioneering new business opportunities across retail, wholesale, and direct-to-consumer markets.

In October 2024, Terri Eagle launched The Terri Eagle Group, a business advisory firm. As the lead strategist, Terri and her team of experienced professionals specialize in creating tailored strategies for growth, branding, marketing, and operations to help businesses thrive and reach their full potential.

Prior to this, Terri held impactful CEO, COO, and senior executive roles with renowned brands such as L'Oréal, Montblanc, David Yurman, John Hardy, Schumacher, and Morilee, where she led successful sales, marketing, and operations strategies that engaged department stores, specialty retailers, company-owned retail stores, and DTC channels alike.

Terri's commitment to mentoring extends beyond business strategies. She's known for surprising her teams with thoughtful gestures that reflect her dedication to their growth and well-being. Both seasoned professionals and emerging leaders seek her guidance for insights on career development and authentic leadership.

Terri lives in New York City with her husband, Bart, and their puppy, Kazzy. In her spare time, she enjoys biking, entertaining friends and family, and exploring new destinations around the world!

CONTACT

If you would like to connect with Terri or are interested in working with The Terri Eagle Group, please scan the QR code below to get in touch with Terri and Terri's team!

GALLERY

My Loving Parents

Dad & Mom—true love & best friends

Dad's Puyallup Fair ribbons for his dahlias

My dad—dahlia garden

Bill—the best dad

My lovely mom, Neva

My dad is #1

From Cheerleader to CEO!

Top of the squad!

Halftime performance

Cascade Bruins cheer squad

Terri & Lael: Best Friends Since High School

Graduation flight to Hawaii

Waikiki Beach, Hawaii

Seattle to New York never held us back

Fabulous Friends

Tour de Bart with besties Alan & Holly—Hamptons, NY

"Anguilla Refugees" Christine, Donna, Bart, Lou, Terri, & Steve

I luv Adele & Susan & Deb

Donna & Lou Cona enjoying Bart's tiki bar!

My dearest Lou Cona in Rome

Auntie Lael loves niece Kazzy

Amy & Gary Churgin, lots of fun times together!

Kazzy luvs Maddie

My favorite hobby—entertaining friends

Susan Pikitch—memories of 30+ years

Molly—fabulous friend of 20+ years

Timothy Corrigan—friends forever

Susan & Chet Borgida—treasured friends

Andy & Michelle Levine—cherished friends

Family Time!

Lindsay Bridal Shower

Alanna Bridal Shower

Alan & Carol—Napa, CA

Cutest nieces and nephews ever!

Jasper & Pearl summertime fun!

Jasper & Pearl & Kazzy

Celebrating with Lindsay, Robbie, & Benji

Ellie, future rockstar

All together now!

Terri & Bart: Thirty Years Together!

Terri & Bart 11/14/1993 "wedding bliss"

30th anniversay vow renewal Las Vegas

Life is a beach! Cheers to Anguilla!

Bart & his true love, his bike

Cheers to LUV!

We Love Music!

TROMBONE SHORTY, "Pier 17 NYC"

Bruce on Broadway! NYC

Gene Casey "Rocks" New Years Eve NYC

Omari Banks "Anguilla Life is Great!"

Business Celebrations & Great Memories over the Years!

Terri—1st career start!

Terri & Gloria Vanderbilt—Glorious Tour

Statue of Liberty, New York, NY—Living My Dream

David Yurman X me X Evan Yurman. "Hampton Classic celebration"

The Oscars—thanks Lou!

Susie Kimball—awesome work bestie!

Tracy Squillante, marekting maven and fabulous friend

GMA!

Happy Birthday, Surim Campos! July 1

Suly Yu welcomes baby girl, Norah

The Blechman Family. Business + Friendship = great times

Rebecca Kimura, special friend & dynamic businesswoman

Grand Adventures!

Backroads, San Juan Islands, WA

Backroads, best R&R ever!

Fur Babies

Nikki, our first doggie!

Zoe—12 years of sweetness

Kazzy—"Riding in Style"